Creative
HEIRLOOM
TREASURES

by Kaylene Evans

A J.B. Fairfax Press Publication

CONTENTS

FOREWORD

It is with great pride and love that I dedicate this book to my dear friend Shirley
and my treasured mother Ellen.

EDITORIAL
Managing Editor: Judy Poulos
Editorial Assistant: Gillian Gilett
Editorial Coordinator: Margaret Kelly
Photography: Andre Martin
Styling: Kathy Tripp
Illustrations: Lesley Griffith

DESIGN AND PRODUCTION
Manager: Anna Maguire
Design: Jenny Nossal
Cover Design: Jenny Pace

Production Artist: Lulu Dougherty
Design & Production Coordinator:
Cheryl Dubyk-Yates

Published by J.B. Fairfax Press Pty Limited
80-82 McLachlan Ave
Rushcutters Bay NSW, 2011 Australia
A.C.N. 003 738 430

Formatted by J.B. Fairfax Press Pty Limited

Printed by Toppan Printing Company,
Singapore

JBFP 467

CREATIVE HEIRLOOM TREASURES
ISBN 1 86343 296 5

INTRODUCTION

Although I have always enjoyed various hobbies and crafts, I have only been embroidering for about seven years. Except for guidance from two very talented friends in the early days, I am totally self-taught. I am not an 'expert', but I do strive to pass on all that I know and have learned about embroidery.

My main wish is, through this book, to share my love for fine embroidery. I have never enjoyed such pleasure, fulfilment and relaxation from any other activity as I have from embroidery. It is my passion and is now my business and an important part of my life.

I hope I can entice you to embroider pieces from my book and that you will feel the fulfilment of knowing your work will become one of your family's treasured heirlooms.

For those who are just beginning, I urge you with all my heart to take the time to learn as much as you can and to persevere. I assure you, you will be rewarded with years of contentment and happiness.

KAE

EMBROIDERY GUIDE

FORGET-ME-NOT

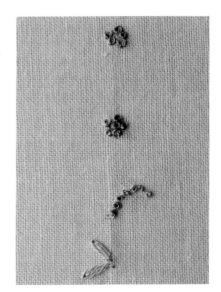

Forget-me-nots are great for filling in gaps and for bringing a design together. You may not always have room for the whole flower; in that case, use only three Blue French knots with a Gold centre. Tuck these half flowers in where they are needed.

 Using a straw needle and Blue thread, place five French knots in a close circle. One twist around the needle will produce a very small flower; two twists around the needle is a nice size.

 Place a Gold French knot (of the same number of twists as the petals) in the centre.

 Forget-me-not seed pods are a series of French knots, graduating from two twists around the needle to one twist around the needle.

 The leaves are long lazy daisy stitches with a straight stitch inside.

FRENCH KNOT FLOWER OR SINGLE ROSE

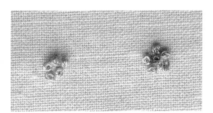

 Using a straw needle, embroider five French knots in a close circle. Use two or three twists around the needle, depending on the size of flower you require.

Work a Gold French knot of the same number of twists around the needle in the centre.

DAISY

For larger daisies, thread up two strands of cotton in the colour of your choice.

Using a crewel needle, work a circle of five or seven petals in lazy daisy stitch. Always have an odd number of petals.

Using two strands of Gold, work a French knot of one twist around the needle in the centre. Work two twists for the larger daisies.

Place a straight stitch inside the petals, if desired.

If there is room for only a half flower, work three lazy daisy stitches with a Gold centre.

GERANIUM OR CYCLAMEN

 Using a crewel needle and one strand of Medium Green, embroider the leaves in buttonhole stitch, working approximately three-quarters of a circle.

 Work two or three straight stitches, then place a lazy daisy stitch at the top in your chosen colour. Add a few extra lazy daisy stitches if you wish.

DAISY BUSH

Lightly trace the outline of the main stems onto the fabric.

Using a crewel needle and one strand of Medium Olive Green, embroider the outline, including the smaller stems, in feather stitch.

Using two strands of White or Ecru (or the colour of your choice) and lazy daisy stitch, embroider tiny daisies all over the bush. For a small bush, work flowers with five petals.

Using one strand of Green, fill in around the flowers and the outer edge of the bush with tiny straight stitches. It does not matter what direction you work the stitches amongst the flowers. Fill in until there are no gaps left.

LEAVES

LAZY DAISY LEAVES
Use one or two strands of thread, depending on the size of the leaf.

Using a crewel needle, embroider three lazy daisy stitches as shown.

Work a straight stitch inside the lazy daisy stitch, if desired.

TINY LAZY DAISY LEAVES

These are used mainly for wisteria or the outer edges of rose bushes. They can also be used to create the illusion of ferns.

Embroider five or seven lazy daisy stitches as shown. These are too small to place a straight stitch inside. Link the leaves with tiny back stitches.

BULLION LEAVES

Using a straw needle and one strand of thread, embroider two bullions, side by side and coming to the same point at the tip. Embroider the leaves in groups of three as shown.

For very small roses, you will need only one bullion for each leaf. Embroider them in groups of three and link them together with tiny back stitches.

RIBBON LEAVES

Using a chenille needle, work the leaves in ribbon stitch in groups of three, as shown.

WISTERIA

Using a straw needle and one strand of Mauve, work French knots of two twists around the needle for the top of the flower, reducing to French knots of one twist around the needle for the bottom. Towards the bottom, you can include a few French knots in a slightly darker shade.

Using a crewel needle, work the leaves in lazy daisy stitches in one strand of Medium or Light to Medium Green. For the smaller leaves, work five or seven tiny lazy daisy stitches.

For smaller leaves, use only three lazy daisy stitches.

For very small wisteria blossoms, work all the French knots with one twist around the needle.

PANSY

The pansies shown in this book are worked in long and short satin stitch, or buttonhole stitch for the tiny pansies.

Using a crewel needle, stitch the two back petals first, beginning with the darkest colour on the left and a slightly lighter shade on the right. Work the stitches in the direction shown.

Work the next two petals in a contrasting colour.

Stitch the front petal in a lighter shade of the contrasting colour or another colour altogether.

Work the 'face' in straight stitches in Black or the colour of your choice. Vary the length of the stitches to give a whiskery effect.

For the small pansies, place a French knot of one twist around the needle in Gold in the centre.

For the pansies in Treasured Times on page 34, place three or four buttonhole stitches in Gold in the centre with a Maroon or Plum French knot above.

Remember: the smaller the flower, the less detail you need to include.

PANSY BUD

Work this in the same stitches as for the full pansy flower. Use a darker shade for the back petal and a lighter shade for the front petal, then work two tiny lazy daisy stitches in Medium Green at the top of the bud. Work the stems in stem stitch or back stitch.

For the leaves, outline them with tiny back stitches, then fill in with satin stitch using a Medium Green at the top, graduating to a lighter Green at the tip.

FOXGLOVE

Using a crewel needle and two strands of thread, begin with four or five lazy daisy stitches in Medium Green for the leaves. Place a straight stitch inside each lazy daisy stitch.

Work another row of lazy daisy stitches above the first row, with a straight stitch inside.

Using a colour of your choice, work the flowers in lazy daisy stitch. Add a straight stitch inside, if you wish.

Using a straw needle and the same colour as for the flowers, work two or three French knots reducing from two to one twists around the needle, at the top.

LAVENDER BUSH

Draw the outline of the lavender bush, then stitch it in feather stitch in one strand of a Light Grey/Green using a crewel needle.

Using a straw needle and one strand of Mauve thread, place a bullion at the top of each feather stitch and wherever there is room. The size of the bullion will depend on the size of the bush. Use 2 mm ($^1/_8$ in) for the smaller ones and 3 mm ($^3/_{16}$ in) for the larger ones. Fill in around the flowers with tiny straight stitches in any direction, using the Light Grey/Green.

BUNCH OF LAVENDER

Work two or three lines of feather stitch. Place a bullion on each tip and wherever there is room. Fill in with straight stitches as for the bush.

Work the stems in stem stitch.

Tie a tiny six-strand bow and stitch it in place with a French knot.

FILL-IN LAVENDER

Place Mauve bullion stitches wherever they are needed and place straight stitches between the bullions.

FILL-IN FLOWERS

These little flowers, worked in a series of closely packed French knots using a straw needle, are wonderful for cottage garden embroidery. The French knots give the illusion of a variety of flowers, depending on the colour chosen. For example, if you work them in Blue, they look like delphiniums; if you work them in Pink, they look like hollyhocks; if you work them in Green on a garden wall, they look like a creeper.

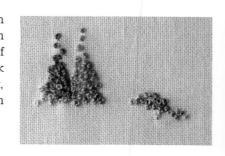

HOLLYHOCK

Using a crewel needle, work the flowers and leaves, in one strand, in buttonhole stitches placed very close together. Stitching into the same hole each time will give the flower a lovely centre. If you wish to stitch a definite centre, add a French knot of one twist around the needle in Gold or the colour of your choice, for the centre.

Begin by embroidering the leaves, working the leaves sitting behind in a darker Green and the leaves sitting on top in a lighter Green. Place partial leaves up the sides of the flower stalks.

Embroider the flowers, starting at the top; this way, the flower at the front will sit nicely on the one behind. Near the top, work a half flower, then French knots reducing from two twists to one twist around a straw needle.

On each side of the half flower, place a tiny Green lazy daisy stitch, then work a couple of Green French knots among the others.

BULLION ROSE 1

Note: See the bullion tips on page 77.

Using a straw needle and one strand of the darkest shade, work three bullions close together for the centre.

Using a shade or two lighter, place a bullion on each side of the centre, coming to a centre point as shown.

Using the same shade, place another pair of bullions on either side, and one bullion across the base of the rose. Add extra wraps to allow for the curve.

BULLION ROSE LEAF

Using a straw needle and Medium Green, embroider two bullions close together for each leaf, coming to a point at the tip. Place the leaves in groups of three.

For the outer leaves on bushes and very tiny designs, work the leaves in single small bullions.

Stems are worked in either stem or back stitch, depending on the size of the flowers.

BULLION ROSE BUD

Using a straw needle, place one, two or three bullions, side by side.

Using a crewel needle and one or two strands of Medium Green (depending on the size required), work a fly stitch around the bullion stitches.

Note: If you can't fit a full rose, don't worry – just do as many bullions as will fit into the space.

9

BULLION ROSE 2

When choosing colours for bullion roses, try to keep about two shades difference – enough to blend the shades, but not a strong contrast.

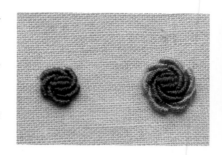

 Using a straw needle and the darkest colour, work three bullions side by side for the centre.

 Change to a medium shade and, working anticlockwise, place five bullions around the centre as shown.

Using the lightest shade, work approximately seven bullions around the first round.

Work the leaves and buds the same as for Bullion Rose 1.

Note: The roses in the Rose and Wisteria Garland Pillow are worked in two shades instead of three.

RIBBON STEM STITCH ROSE

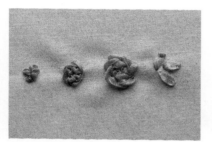

This rose is worked in silk ribbon.

 Using a chenille needle, place three or four French knots close together for the centre.

 Work a row of stem stitches in the same colour around the circle, then work a second row around the first one. Finish off the ribbon on the back of the work and stitch it down with thread.

SPIDER-WEB ROSE

This rose is worked in silk ribbon. Take care when using ribbon; it is very easy to pull the work.

In a single strand of thread in the same colour as the ribbon, work five spokes. Try to space them evenly.

Using a chenille needle and the ribbon, work three French knots of one twist around the needle in the centre of the spokes.

 Come up on the left-hand side of any of the spokes and begin weaving the ribbon over and under, twisting it gently as you go. When the rose is the desired size and the spokes are covered, take the ribbon through to the back and stitch it down with thread.

 The leaves are worked in ribbon stitch.

 The buds are also worked in ribbon stitch with a Green fly stitch in two strands around it, using a crewel needle.

SINGLE OPEN ROSE

 Using a crewel needle, work around the flower in long and short buttonhole stitches.

 Using a shade or two darker, work a few straight stitches of various lengths on each petal. Satin stitch the centre in Gold.

 Work a few tiny Green straight stitches around the centre of the flower. Using the same colour, place a French knot of one twist around the needle in the centre of the centre.

LEAVES

 Work the leaves in long and short satin stitches, placing the darkest colour at the top of the leaf.

BUDS

Work the buds in buttonhole stitch with a Green fly stitch around it. Place two Green lazy daisy stitches at the top of the bud. The stems are worked in stem stitch.

SILK RIBBON ROSE

I have used Vintage Silk Embroidery Ribbons for this rose in the Shadow Box Teddy on page 19, but you could use any 12 mm ($^1/_2$ in) wide silk ribbon. The Vintage silk ribbon is approximately 32 mm ($1^1/_4$ in) wide, so cut it in half, then gather the raw edge.

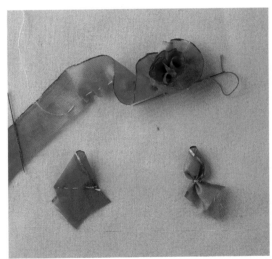

Begin with a piece of ribbon approximately 30 cm (12 in) long. Run a small gathering stitch along the bottom of the ribbon, tapering up to the top edge. Fold down the other edge at an angle of 45 degrees. Roll up the folded edge three or four times and stitch it at the base to secure it. Gather the ribbon a few centimetres (one inch) at a time, folding in the end as you gather. Stitch the base as you go. Gather up the full length of the ribbon and finish off.

For the leaves, cut 7 cm ($2^3/_4$ in) lengths of 12 mm ($^1/_2$ in) wide Green silk ribbon. Fold in the sides as shown. Gather across the base and stitch to secure.
Vintage Silk Ribbon is available from the Judith and Kathryn stand at major craft shows.

BIRDS

Embroider birds in any colour you choose; Blue is very popular. Outline the shape of the bird in back stitch using a crewel needle. Fill in the outline in long and short satin stitches, overlapping the stitches to prevent a ridge forming.

Using a straw needle, place a French knot of one wrap around the needle in Black for the eye. Work the beak in two straight stitches in Gold.

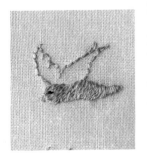

ROSE BUSH

Begin by drawing the outline of the bush.

Embroider the roses and leaves in the colours of your choice.

Using a straw needle, fill in around the roses with French knots, varying from one to two twists around the needle in two or three shades of Green. Add rose buds and lazy daisy leaves. If you embroider the lazy daisy leaves in a plum shade, it gives the illusion of new growth.

Outline the stem in stem stitch in two shades of Brown. Give the stem a little character by making it slightly crooked. When embroidering very small rose bushes, work just a single bullion for the leaves.

VIOLET

Use a crewel needle and one or two strands depending on the size desired.

Begin with two lazy daisy stitches at the top of the flower.

Work the bottom of the flower in buttonhole stitches, placed close together.

Place a lazy daisy stitch on both sides of the centre. Work a straight stitch inside each lazy daisy stitch.

In the centre, work a Gold French knot of one twist around a straw needle.

VIOLET BUD

Work two lazy daisy stitches in Mauve.

Work two lazy daisy stitches in Medium Green.

Work the stems in stem stitch or tiny back stitches.

VIOLET LEAF

Work the leaves in one strand of Medium Green and buttonhole stitch. Work approximately three-quarters of a circle for each leaf.

12

BOWS

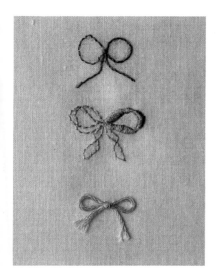

Bows are wonderful, particularly for finishing and adding a special touch to a piece of embroidery.

A fine bow is worked in tiny back stitches using a crewel needle, then whipped. Place a French knot of one twist around the needle in the centre.

A more generous bow is satin stitched, outlined in back stitches if you like.
This tiny bow is a cutie. Make it by tying six strands of thread into a small bow and stitching it into place with a French knot.

TASSELS

Tassels worked in Gold or Silver make a wonderful contrast with the coloured threads.

 Using a crewel needle and one strand, work the top of the tassel in satin stitch.

 Work the skirt of the tassel in long and short straight stitches.

Work two satin stitches across, between the top and the skirt.

Work the cord in tiny chain stitches.

IRIS

 Using a crewel needle, work the iris flowers as upside-down fly stitches with a lazy daisy stitch on top. Add a straight stitch inside the lazy daisy stitch, if you wish, and a Gold French knot in the centre.

 Work the leaves as straight stitches in a Grey/Green shade, placing a long stitch in the centre and a shorter stitch on each side. The stems are also straight stitches.

 Work a clump of stems and leaves, then embroider the flowers at the top of the stems.

MAY SUNSHINE PILLOW

This charming embroidery with its sentimental message would look equally pleasing as a framed picture.

MATERIALS

70 cm (28 in) of ivory homespun cotton

1 m (1¹/₈ yd) of 4 cm (1¹/₂ in) wide lace edging

Crewel needle, size 10

Straw needle, size 10

Sewing thread to match the fabric

Embroidery hoop

Pillow insert, 16 cm x 30 cm (6 in x 12 in)

Stranded Cotton:

DMC	Madeira
504	1701
503	1702
932	1710
316	0809
778	0808
Ecru	Ecru
414	1801
834	2204

Note: this piece has been worked in Madeira Stranded Cotton.

PREPARATION

See the tracing and embroidery designs on the Pull Out Pattern Sheet.

STEP ONE

Cut an 18 cm (7 in) strip across the width of the fabric. From the strip cut two pieces each 18 cm x 32 cm (7 in x 12¹/₂ in) for the front and back of the pillow. Cut two strips 15 cm x 80 cm (6 in x 32 in) and two strips 15 cm x 50 cm (7 in x 20 in) for the ruffle.

STEP TWO

Trace the embroidery design onto the front piece, using the method described on page 79. You can trace the motto, but it is far better to use your own writing. It can be quite difficult at first, but it is well worth persevering.

EMBROIDERY

Note: Embroider the flowers following the Embroidery Guide on page 5 and the Stitch Guide on page 77. All the embroidery is worked in one strand unless stated otherwise.

STEP ONE

Using the crewel needle and 0808, embroider the roses and rose buds in long and short buttonhole stitch. Using 0809, work long and short straight stitches on each petal. Using 2204 satin stitch the centres. Finally, using 1701 work a French knot of one twist around the needle in the centre of the centre. Using 1701 work a few tiny straight stitches around the centre of the flower. Work the leaves in long and short satin stitch using 1701 and 1702, placing the darker colour at the top.

STEP TWO

Using the straw needle, embroider the single roses in French knots of three twists around the needle, using Ecru.

Create shading on the petals

Work tiny French knots in 2204 for the centres. Work the forget-me-nots in French knots of one twist around the needle using 1710. Finally, work the tiny leaves in lazy daisy stitches in 1701.

STEP THREE

Embroider the scrolls in tiny back stitches in 1801 with a French knot of one twist around the crewel needle in each square, in the same colour.

STEP FOUR

Using the hoop, embroider the motto in tiny back stitches in 1801, then embroider your name and the date.

MAKING UP

STEP ONE

Press the ruffle strips over double with the wrong sides facing. Open out the strips and pin them together at the corners in perfect diagonals up to the pressed line. Stitch the four corner seams and trim. Fold the ruffles over double so the right sides are facing. Pin, sew and trim the second part of the corner seams as before. Turn the ruffle right side out. Gather the raw edges. Baste the lace edging to the ruffle. Pin and baste the ruffle to the pillow front. Take care not to place too much fullness at the mitred corners.

STEP TWO

Place the front and back of the pillow together with the right sides facing, the raw edges even and the ruffle in between. Stitch through all layers, leaving a 15 cm (6 in) opening in one long side. Place the insert inside the cover and slipstitch the opening closed.

May sunshine light
Your path through life

FLOWER SAMPLER

A sampler is always a delight to own and display. The flower designs in this pretty flower sampler can all be used separately or in groups in many different ways.

MATERIALS

45 cm (18 in) square of linen
Crewel needle, size 10
Straw needle, size 10
Stranded Cotton:

DMC	MADEIRA
503	1702
502	1703
504	1701
White	White
3042	0807
3041	0806
745	0111
898	2006
3052	1509
729	2209
902	0601
315	0810
316	0809
778	0808
932	1710
3024	1901
Black	Black

Note: this piece has been worked in Madeira Stranded Cotton.

PREPARATION

See the tracing and the embroidery designs on the Pull Out Pattern Sheet.

Trace the design onto the centre of the linen using the method described on page 79.

EMBROIDERY

Note: Embroider the flowers following the Embroidery Guide on page 5 and the Stitch Guide on page 77. All the embroidery is worked in one strand unless stated otherwise. You may prefer to embroider the six rows of flowers first, then the bluebirds and hanging basket. For each group of flowers, embroider the main flowers first, then fill in with the leaves, daisies and forget-me-nots.

STEP ONE

Using the photograph as a guide and following the embroidery design, begin working at the top with the first row. Using the straw needle and 0601 and beginning each rose with a 3 mm ($^3/_{16}$ in) long bullion, place three bullions for the centre. Change to 0810 and embroider approximately five bullions around the centre. Work the outer circle of bullions in 0808. Embroider the buds in 0810 for the centre and 0808 for the outer petals. Work the fly stitch around the bud in 1702.

Using the straw needle, embroider the leaves in bullion stitch, using 1702.

Using the crewel needle and two strands of White, embroider half daisies with three petals. Work a French knot of two twists around the needle in the centre, using 2209.

Using the straw needle, embroider the forget-me-nots in 1710 and 2209 for the centres.

Massed flowers create a charming texture

STEP TWO

For the second row, using the crewel needle and two strands of White, embroider the daisies in lazy daisy stitch. Work a French knot of two twists around the needle in 2209 for the centre. Using 1509, work straight stitches between the daisies to give the illusion of leaves.

Using the straw needle and 1710, embroider the forget-me-nots in French knots of one twist around the needle. Work the centre in 2209.

STEP THREE

Using the crewel needle and two strands of thread, embroider the violets, using 0806 for the dark flowers and 0807 for the light ones. Work French knots in the centre using 2209.

Using the crewel needle and 1702, work the leaves in half-buttonhole stitches.

Embroider the buds in 0806 and the stems in stem stitch, using 1702. Using the straw needle and 1710, work the forget-me-nots in French knots of one twist around the needle using 1710 and 2209 for the centre.

STEP FOUR

Using the crewel needle and 1710, embroider the bluebirds in long and short, overlapping satin stitches to ensure there are no ridges. When the outline of the bird is filled in, using the straw needle, work a French knot of

Combine forget-me-nots and daisies

one twist around the needle in Black for the eye. Work the beak with two straight stitches in 2209.

STEP FIVE

For the hanging basket, using the crewel needle, work the chains in tiny straight stitches and the bowl of the basket in stem stitch in 1901.

Using the straw needle and 0809, embroider the rose centres, beginning with a 4 mm (^{3}/$_{16}$ in) bullion. Using 0808, embroider the rest of the rose petals. Using the crewel needle and 0111, embroider the single roses in French knots of two twists around the needle. Work a French knot in 2209 for the centre. Using the straw needle and 1702, embroider the rose leaves.

Using the crewel needle and 0806, embroider the half violets.

Using the straw needle and 0809, embroider the rose buds with a fly stitch in 1702 around each one.

Using the straw needle, fill in with forget-me-nots in French knots of one twist around the needle using 1710 for the flowers and the centres in 2209. Place these around the larger flowers and in any bare spots.

Using the crewel needle and 1701, work tiny lazy daisy stitch leaves around the outer edge of the basket.

Using the crewel needle and 1901, embroider your initials and the date.

STEP SIX

Using the crewel needle and 2209, embroider the back two open roses using long and short buttonhole stitches. Using 1703, work a few tiny straight stitches around the centre. Using 1703, work a French knot of two twists around the needle in the centre. Using the crewel needle and 2006, embroider the three front open roses.

Using the straw needle and 1703, embroider the leaves in bullion stitches.

Using the crewel needle, embroider the buds in buttonhole stitches using 2006. Work a fly stitch around each bud using 1703.

Using the straw needle and 1710, work French knots of one twist around the needle for the forget-me-nots. Work the centres in 2209.

STEP SEVEN

Using the straw needle and 0809, embroider the roses. Begin each rose with a 4 mm (^{3}/$_{16}$ in) bullion. Change to 0808 and work the rest of the petals.

Using the straw needle and 1702, embroider the bullion leaves.

Using the straw needle and 0809, work the rose buds in two bullion stitches with a fly stitch around each one in 1702. Using the straw needle and 1710, work French knots of one twist around the needle for the forget-me-nots. Work the centres in 2209.

STEP EIGHT

Using the crewel needle and long and short buttonhole stitches, embroider the centre pansy first, using 0806 for the back petal, 2209 for the petal to the right of it, 0807 for the next two petals and 0111 for the front petal. Work the face in 0806 and the centre in 2209.

Work the pansy on the right in the same way, using 0806, 0807 and 2006. Use 0806 for the face and 2209 for the French knot in the centre.

Work the pansy on the left in the same way using 0806, 2006 and 0807. Use 0806 for the face and 2209 for the French knot in the centre.

Using the crewel needle, work the buds at the top in buttonhole stitches in 0807 and the ones at the sides in 0806.

Work the stems in 1509 and the leaves in long and short satin stitches, using the same colour.

Using the straw needle and 1710, work the forget-me-nots in French knots of one twist around the needle. Work the centres in 2209.

STEP NINE

For the bow, tie six strands of cotton into a small bow and stitch it in place with tiny straight stitches in the same colour. Finish the bow with a French knot of one twist in the centre.

SHADOW BOX TEDDY

This is intended to be an inspirational piece, rather than one to be copied exactly. Let your heart rule your head and make this a piece you truly love working on. Add as much or as little lace and trinkets as you wish. Remember, these shadow boxes are meant to be 'over the top'.

MATERIALS

Acid-free double-sided tape
20 cm x 25 cm (8 in x 10 in) photo-
    graph (sepia is preferable)
60 cm (24 in) square of backing
    fabric, such as damask, silk or
    furnishing fabric
Sentimental cards of your choice
    (I used old baby cards)
Small lace motifs
Larger lace motifs or pieces of lace
    (tea- or coffee-dyed)
Buttons and charms
Old brooches with the backs
    removed
Brass corner for the photograph
Vintage Silk Embroidery Ribbon:
    Gold, Burgundy, Dark Plum
Two pieces of cream wool felt, each
    18 cm x 25 cm (7 in x 10 in)
Polyester filling
Small heart charm
Small bird charm
25 cm (10 in) of cream double-sided
    satin ribbon for bow
Madeira Metallic Embroidery
    Thread, Gold 3004
Ordinary sewing thread
Stranded cotton:

DMC	MADEIRA
224	0813
225	0814
523	1512
524	1511
676	0210
677	2207
712	2101
729	2209
738	2013
775	0108
950	2309
3774	0306

Note: This piece has been worked in DMC Stranded Cotton.

TEDDY TO LOVE

Note: Embroider the flowers and the tassels following the Embroidery Guide on page 5 and the Stitch Guide on page 77. All the embroidery is worked in one strand unless stated otherwise.

See the pattern and the embroidery design for the teddy on the Pull Out Pattern Sheet.

See the pattern and the embroidery design for the teddy on the Pull Out Pattern Sheet.

following the Embroidery Guide on page 5 and the Stitch Guide on page 77.

STEP ONE

Trace the teddy pattern and transfer it to one piece of the cream wool felt with a dotted line. Do not cut it out at this stage. Trace the embroidery design onto this piece for the front of the teddy.

STEP TWO

On the front teddy, using the straw needle, embroider the large roses on the heart first, beginning each rose with a bullion stitch 3 mm ($^3/_{16}$ in) long for the centre of the roses. Work the pink rose centres in 224 and the petals

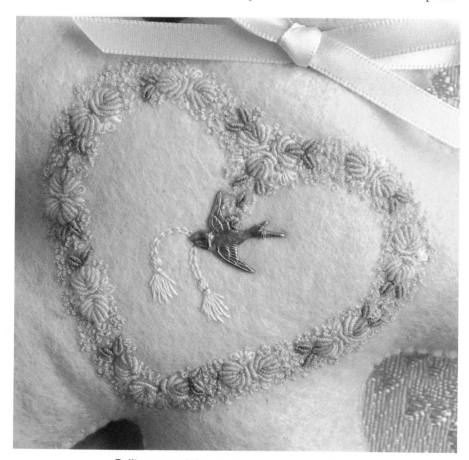

Bullion roses define the heart-shaped embroidery

19

in 225; the lemon rose centres in 676 and the petals in 677; the peach rose centres in 950 and the petals in 3774.

Embroider the leaves using one bullion each of 523 and 524, with the lighter shade on top. Fill in with a tiny three-petal daisy in 712 on each side of the roses and tiny forget-me-nots in 775 with 729 centres, keeping an even heart-shape.

STEP THREE

Embroider the roses, daisies, leaves and forget-me-nots on the right leg and the small posy on the left leg. Work tiny forget-me-nots around roses. Using the straw needle, embroider two-bullion buds in 676, 3774 and 224 with a fly stitch around each bud in 523. Work the stems in straight stitches.

STEP FOUR

Tie a small six-strand bow in 775 and stitch it in place on the right leg. Stitch the heart charm to the bow with the metallic thread.

STEP FIVE

Using the crewel needle and 775, outline the eyes in tiny back stitches, then fill in with satin stitch. Outline the nose and mouth in tiny back stitches in 738, then fill in the nose with satin stitch.

STEP SIX

Sit the small bird charm in position and place a dot where the tassel will pass through the bird's beak. Using the crewel needle and 775, chain stitch the cord, passing through this point. Stitch a tassel at each end of the cord.

STEP SEVEN

Place the two pieces of wool felt together with the embroidery facing outwards. Baste them together just inside the outline, then cut them out. Take care to cut slowly to retain a nice rounded shape. With the basting still in place, buttonhole stitch the two pieces together, beginning at the bottom and working up the left side. Keep the blanket stitches approximately 2 mm (^{1}/8 in) apart. When you

reach the top of the left arm, remove the basting in this area and push some of the filling inside this half of the teddy. Continue stitching around the teddy until you reach the bottom of the right leg. Remove the basting in this section and stuff the right arm and leg. Finish stuffing the teddy, keeping it quite even and taking care not to overstuff in case he bursts. Continue stitching around the right leg until you are approximately 2 cm (^{3}/4 in) from where you began. Finish stuffing the right leg, then finish the buttonhole stitching. Tie a ribbon bow around teddy's neck.

MAKING UP

STEP ONE

Using acid-free double-sided tape, cover the back of the photograph, taking it right out to the sides. Place the photograph in position on the backing fabric and press down firmly.

STEP TWO

Stitch the lace or lace motifs in the left corner. You may enjoy putting the lace all around the photograph, as in the wedding piece on page 69.

STEP THREE

Make silk ribbon roses and leaves and stitch them into position (see pages 10–11). Stitch the buttons, brass photo corner, charms and brooches and any other trinkets into position.

STEP FOUR

Attach the cards with double-sided tape as for the photograph. I placed a little double-sided tape under the crocheted motif on the cards, as well. You may stitch through cards and photograph, if you prefer.

STEP FIVE

Place the teddy into position, using the double-sided tape to attach it on the photograph. At the back, catch it on the fabric side with straight stitches.

STEP SIX

When you are happy with your arrangement, ask your framer to make a box frame to protect your treasures.

Vintage silk ribbon and vintage silk spindle are available from Judith and Kathryn Design stands at major craft and needlework shows.

Gentle shading is preferable to strong contrast

SILHOUETTE PILLOW

This delightful silk pillow has a very Victorian look.
It would be equally appealing if it was framed,
as silhouettes often were in those times.

MATERIALS

25 cm (10 in) square of antique gold
  silk for the pillow front
50 cm (20 in) of antique gold silk for
  the pillow back and ruffle
Four purchased tassels
25 cm (10 in) pillow insert
Crewel needle, size 10
Straw needle, size 10
Stranded cotton:

DMC	Madeira
504	1701
503	1702
502	1703
3041	0806
3042	0807
902	0601
315	0810
729	2209
781	2213
310	Black

Note: This piece has been worked in
Madeira Stranded Cotton.

PREPARATION

See the tracing and the embroidery
designs on this page.

  Trace the design onto the pillow
front using the method described on
page 79.

EMBROIDERY

Note: Embroider the flowers following
the Embroidery Guide on page 5 and
the Stitch Guide on page 77. All the
embroidery is worked in one strand
unless stated otherwise.

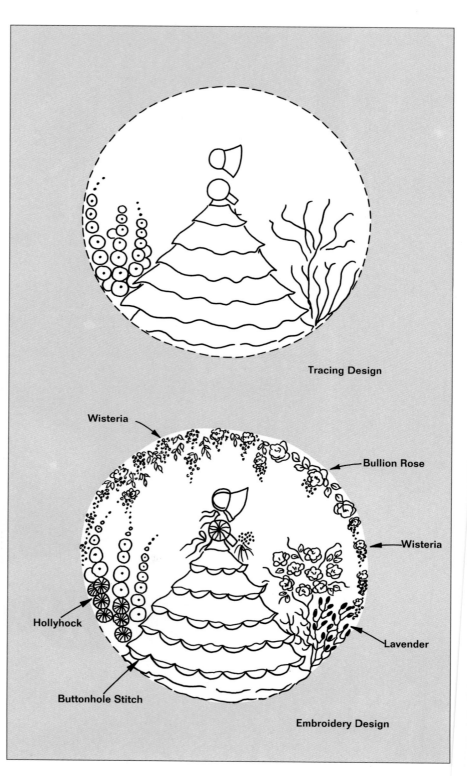

Tracing Design

Wisteria

Bullion Rose

Wisteria

Lavender

Hollyhock

Buttonhole Stitch

Embroidery Design

23

STEP ONE

Using the crewel needle, commence by embroidering the lady, working the dress and bonnet in scallops of buttonhole stitch in Black. Try to follow the curve of each layer. The top of the sleeve is a circle of Black buttonhole stitches. Embroider the base of the sleeve in satin stitch.

STEP TWO

Following the embroidery design and using the straw needle, work the rose bush, placing the flowers in first, each with a bullion stitch centre approximately 2 mm ($^1/_8$ in) long. Use 0601 for the centre and 0810 for the outer petals. Embroider the leaves around the outer edge in bullion stitches in 1702. Fill in between the roses with French knots of one twist around the needle in 1701, 1702 and 1703. Finally, add the rose buds in 0601 with a fly stitch in 1702 around each bud.

STEP THREE

Using the crewel needle, work the lavender bush by outlining the tracing with feather stitch in 1701. Using the straw needle and 0807, work a bullion on each tip and any other areas you wish. Fill in any bare spots with straight stitches in any direction in 1701.

STEP FOUR

Using the crewel needle, work the hollyhocks in buttonhole stitch in 0601, 0810 and 2209, finishing at the top with two French knots of two twists each, then one or two French knots of one twist. Place tiny lazy daisy stitches in 1702 on each side of the top flower. Work the leaves in buttonhole stitch in 1702 and 1703.

STEP FIVE

Using the straw needle, embroider the wisteria flowers in 0806, keeping them close to the outer edge and maintaining the circular shape. Use only one twist around the needle for these flowers. Using the crewel needle, embroider the leaves in tiny lazy daisy stitches in 1702.

STEP SIX

Using the straw needle, embroider the roses close to the edge of the circle, beginning each one with a 3 mm ($^3/_{16}$ in) bullion in the centre. Work the rose centres in 2213 and the outer petals 2209. Embroider the leaves in 1702. Work the buds in bullion stitches in 2209 with a fly stitch surrounding each bud in 1702.

STEP SEVEN

For the lady's bouquet, using the straw needle, work a few French knots in the colours of your choice, working tiny straight stitches for the stems in 1702. Stitch the hair and the bow using the crewel needle and tiny back stitches in Black.

MAKING UP

STEP ONE

From the piece of antique gold silk, cut a 25 cm (10 in) square for the pillow back and four 12 cm (4$^3/_4$ in) wide strips across the width of the fabric to join together for the ruffle.

STEP TWO

Press the ruffle strips over double with the wrong sides facing. Open out the strips and pin them together at the corners in perfect diagonals, pinning up only to the pressed line. Stitch the four corner seams and trim the excess fabric. Fold the ruffles over double so the right sides are facing. Pin, sew and trim the second part of the four corner seams as before. Turn the ruffle right side out. Gather the raw edges to fit around the pillow front. Pin and baste the tassels at the corners.

STEP THREE

Pin and baste the ruffle to the pillow front, placing the mitres at the corners of the pillow. Take care not to place too much fullness at the mitred corners.

STEP FOUR

Place the front and back of the pillow together with the right sides facing, the raw edges even and the ruffle sandwiched in between. Stitch through all layers, leaving a 15 cm (6 in) opening in one side. Place the pillow insert inside the cover and stitch the opening closed with small hand stitches.

Contrast the dark silhouette with colourful flowers

MINIATURE GARDEN SCENE

Timeless and appealing, this miniature garden with its
stone wall and tiny flowers is full of charming detail.

Note: If you feel this design is too small for you to work successfully, enlarge it on a photocopier. Work the embroidery in one strand of thread, but work the French knots with two twists around the needle, reducing to one twist.

MATERIALS

30 cm (12 in) square of homespun cotton
Crewel needle, size 10
Straw needle, size 10
Stranded cotton:

DMC	MADEIRA
869	2105
3042	0807
3041	0806
White	White
3052	1509
502	1703
503	1702
677	2207
316	0809
778	0808
832	2202
414	1801
3024	1901

Note: This piece has been worked in Madeira Stranded Cotton.

PREPARATION

See the tracing and the embroidery designs on page 26.

Lightly trace the outline of the major elements in the design, using the method described on page 79.

EMBROIDERY

Note: Embroider the flowers following the Embroidery Guide on Page 5 and the Stitch Guide on page 77. All the embroidery is worked in one strand unless stated otherwise.

STEP ONE

Using the straw needle, commence embroidering the wisteria in 0807 in French knots of one twist around the needle. Using the crewel needle, work the wisteria leaves in tiny lazy daisy stitches in 1702.

STEP TWO

Using the crewel needle, outline the standard rose bush in back stitch in 2105. Fill in the main stem using straight stitches and make the stem appear a little crooked for added character. Using the straw needle, embroider the roses, placing a bullion stitch approximately 2 mm ($^1/_8$ in) long for the centre of each rose. Use 0809 for the centre and 0808 for the outer petals. Embroider the leaves in bullion stitches approximately 2 mm ($^1/_8$ in) long in 1703. Fill in with French knots of one twist around the needle in 1702 and 1703. Embroider the rose buds in 0809 with a fly stitch surround in 1703. Embroider the outer leaves in three single bullions in 1702 and finish off with tiny lazy daisy stitches in 1702.

STEP THREE

Using the crewel needle, outline the daisy bush using feather stitch and 1509. Embroider the tiny daisies with

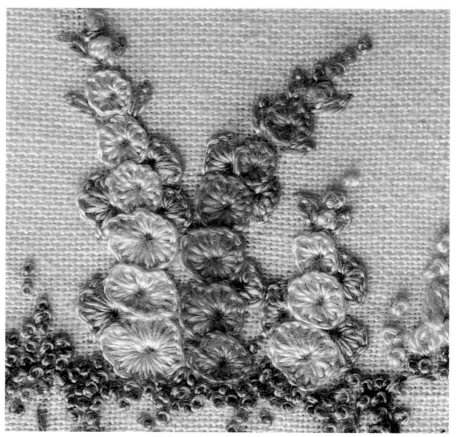

Use French knots to create the illusion of plants and flowers

two petals each in lazy daisy stitches in two strands of White. Using the straw needle, work a French knot in 2207 in the centre of each daisy. Using the crewel needle and 1509, fill in around the flowers and on the edge of the daisy bush with tiny straight stitches in any direction.

STEP FOUR

Using the crewel needle and 1702, outline the lavender bush in feather stitch. Using the straw needle and 0806, embroider tiny bullions around the edge of the bush. This bush has fewer flowers than others. Using the crewel needle and 1702, fill in the bush and around the outside edge with tiny straight stitches in any direction.

STEP FIVE

Using the crewel needle, embroider the hollyhocks on the garden wall in wheels of buttonhole stitches in 0809 and 0808, using the photograph as a guide. Work the leaves in half buttonhole stitches in 1702.

STEP SIX

Using the crewel needle and two strands of thread, embroider the foxgloves on the left of the hollyhocks and between the rose bush and the hollyhocks in lazy daisy stitches in 0809 and 2207. Using the straw needle, embroider the tiny flowers in the right-hand corner with French knots of one twist around the needle in 0806 and 0809.

STEP SEVEN

Using the crewel needle, embroider the clump of irises at the foot of the wall. The straight stitch leaves are worked in 1702 and the flowers are worked in 2207.

STEP EIGHT

Using the straw needle and 1702, 1703, 1509 and 2202, embroider French

knots, all of one twist around the needle, along the top of the wall and tumbling down it. Embroider more French knots in Greens and 2207 along the bottom of the wall.

STEP NINE

Finish by embroidering in tiny back stitches in 1901 any outlines on the wall that are still visible.

STEP TEN

Have the completed embroidery professionally framed. This piece is designed for the mount to be very close to the work.

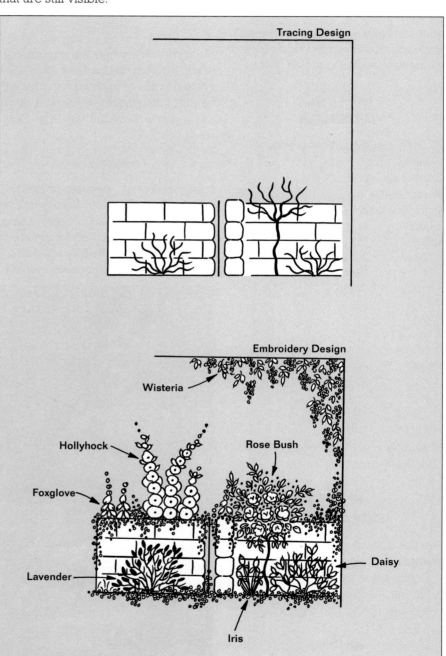

Tracing Design

Embroidery Design

Wisteria

Hollyhock

Foxglove

Rose Bush

Lavender

Daisy

Iris

AFTERNOON TEATIME

**Dainty china on pretty linen are perfectly evoked in this
lovely piece suitable for any room in the house.**

MATERIALS

40 cm (16 in) of crewel linen
Crewel needle, size 10
Straw needle, size 10
Stranded Cotton:

DMC	MADEIRA
Ecru	Ecru
778	0808
503	1702
316	0809
3042	0807
3041	0806
3052	1509
310	Black
932	1710
3023	1902
315	0810
834	2204
3046	2206
677	2207

Note: This piece has been worked in Madeira Stranded Cotton.

PREPARATION

See the tracing and the embroidery designs on the Pull Out Pattern Sheet.

Trace the tracing design onto the linen using the method described on page 79.

EMBROIDERY

Note: Embroider the flowers following the Embroidery Guide on page 5 and the Stitch Guide on page 77. All the embroidery is worked in one strand unless stated otherwise.

STEP ONE

Using the crewel needle, outline the teaset in tiny back stitches in 1902.

STEP TWO

The wallpaper is embroidered in two different stripes. The first is a row of tiny chain stitches in 0808, the second row is worked in feather stitch in 1702 with a tiny bullion rose in 0808 on each tip. Work a fly stitch in 1702 around each rose.

STEP THREE

Using the crewel needle and Ecru, commence embroidering the doily at the centre V-point with a three-quarter circle of buttonhole stitches whose centre is right at the point. Continue working semi-circles of buttonhole stitches on each side for the entire length, placing them approximately 7 mm ($^5/_{16}$ in) apart, then work a row of chain stitch close to the edge. Work random buttonhole stitch circles over the doily, interspersed with random French knots of one twist around the needle.

STEP FOUR

For the runner, begin at the edge and work towards the centre. Using the crewel needle and Ecru, place buttonhole stitch semi-circles as for the doily. Between each pair of circles, embroider a tassel. Finish with a row of chain stitch close to the edge.

STEP FIVE

For the teaset, using the straw needle, work 2.5 mm ($^3/_{16}$ in) bullions for the rose centre on the jug and teapot, then complete the rose. Work the rose centres in 2204 and the petals in 2206. Work the leaves in 2.5 mm ($^3/_{16}$ in) bullions in 1509. For the bullion roses and the leaves on the teacup, make the centre bullions 2 mm ($^1/_8$ in) long. Work random French knots of one twist around the needle in 2206 over all the pieces, except the vase of pansies.

STEP SIX

Using the crewel needle, embroider the pansies and buds in the vase using long and short buttonhole stitches and the following colours:
• For the pansy at the top left and right front: back petals in 0809, side petals in 0808, front petal in 0808 and the face in 0810;
• For the pansy at top right: back petals in 0806, side petals in 0807, front petal in 0807 and the face in Black;
• For the part pansy at the left front: side petals in 2206, front in 2207 and the face in 0806;
• For the pansy in the centre: back petals in 0806, side petals in 0807, front petal in 2207 and the face in 0806.

STEP SEVEN

Fill in with tiny forget-me-nots in French knots of one twist around the needle in 1710 and centres in 2207. Place forget-me-not buds around the edges. Work the pattern on the vase in straight stitches in 1902.

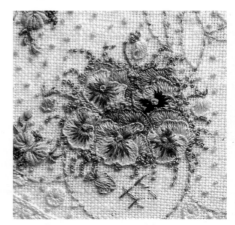

Pansies are a special favourite

BE TRUE

The perfect gift for someone special, this small embroidery embodies the spirit of love and friendship.

MATERIALS

30 cm (12 in) square of ivory home-spun cotton
Crewel needle, size 10
Straw needle, size 10
25 cm (10 in) of 3 mm (³/₁₆ in) wide silk ribbon or satin ribbon, Coffee
Madeira Silk Embroidery Floss, 2209
Stranded Cotton:

DMC	MADEIRA
869	2105
504	1701
902	0601
315	0810
502	1703
Ecru	Ecru
3041	0806
932	1710
729	2209

Note: This piece has been worked in Madeira Stranded Cotton.

PREPARATION

See the tracing and the embroidery designs on this page.

Trace the outline of the embroidery onto the homespun, using the method described on page 79.

EMBROIDERY

Note: Embroider the flowers following the Embroidery Guide on page 5 and the Stitch Guide on page 77. All the embroidery is worked in one strand unless stated otherwise.

STEP ONE

The twisted ribbon is anchored in place with a French knot of one twist around the needle in silk thread. To start, fold the ribbon in half and mark the centre. Starting at the top left-hand corner, stitch down the centre of the ribbon with a French knot. Continue to twist the ribbon at right angles, working to the right, then working down.

STEP TWO

Using the straw needle, embroider the bullion roses, beginning with a bullion stitch 3–4 mm (³/₁₆ in) long for the centre. Work the rose centres in 0601 and the petals in 0810. Embroider the leaves as pairs of bullion stitches in sets of three, using 1703.

STEP THREE

Using the straw needle and Ecru, work the small single roses in French knots of three twists around the needle, centres in 2209. Work the lavender in bullion stitches in 0806 with a straight stitch in 1701 between the bullions. Work the rose buds in 2.5–3 mm (³/₁₆ in) bullion stitches in 0601 with a fly stitch surround in 1703.

STEP FOUR

Using the straw needle, fill in around the design with small forget-me-nots in French knots of two twists around the needle in 1710 with a French knot centre in 2209.

STEP FIVE

Using the crewel needle and the silk thread 2209, embroider the tassels. Using the crewel needle, outline the wording in tiny back stitches in 2105. In the same coloured thread, embroider your name and the date.

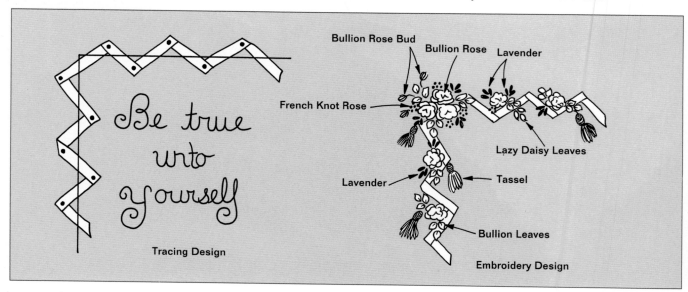

Tracing Design

Bullion Rose Bud
Bullion Rose
Lavender
French Knot Rose
Lazy Daisy Leaves
Lavender
Tassel
Bullion Leaves
Embroidery Design

Be true
unto
yourself

KAE 1996

31

BASKET OF FLOWERS

The charm is in the detail. This miniature would look delightful as part of a group or standing alone on a sideboard easel.

MATERIALS

25 cm (10 in) square of ivory
   dupion silk
Madeira Silk Embroidery Floss:
   0806, 2208, 2207, 0112, 2209,
   2210, 1710, 1703, 1701
4 mm ($^3/_{16}$ in) wide YLI silk ribbon:
   Mauve, Pale Lemon, Green
Straw needle, size 10
Crewel needle, size 10
Chenille needle, size 22
Special button

EMBROIDERY

See the tracing and the embroidery designs on this page.

Note: Embroider the flowers following the Embroidery Guide on page 5 and the Stitch Guide on page 77. All the embroidery is worked in one strand unless stated otherwise.

STEP ONE

Using the crewel needle, work the basket in a basketweave pattern in satin stitch in silk thread, 2209 and 2210. The base is worked in stem stitch and the handle is satin stitched in 2210. The bow is satin stitch in 0806.

STEP TWO

Lightly mark in the ribbon flowers and buds. Using the straw needle, work the bullion roses first with the centres in 2209 and the outer petals in 2207, making the centre bullion approximately 3 mm ($^3/_{16}$ in) long.

STEP THREE

Using the chenille needle, work the three spider-web ribbon roses in the Mauve silk ribbon. Work the buds in

Silk ribbon and stranded cotton combine well

ribbon stitch with a fly stitch surround in 1703.

STEP FOUR

Work the tiny single roses with five French knots of one twist around the needle in the Pale Lemon silk ribbon with a French knot centre of three twists around the needle in 2210.

STEP FIVE

Work the ribbon leaves. Then, using the straw needle and 2208, embroider the rose buds with two bullion stitches, surrounded by fly stitches in 1703.

STEP SIX

Using the straw needle, fill in around the larger flowers with forget-me-nots in French knots in 1710 with French knot centres in 2210, all of one twist around the needle.

STEP SEVEN

Using the crewel needle, work tiny leaves in lazy daisy stitches in 1701 around the outer edge of design, interspersing them with random French knots of one twist around the needle in 0112. Stitch the button in place.

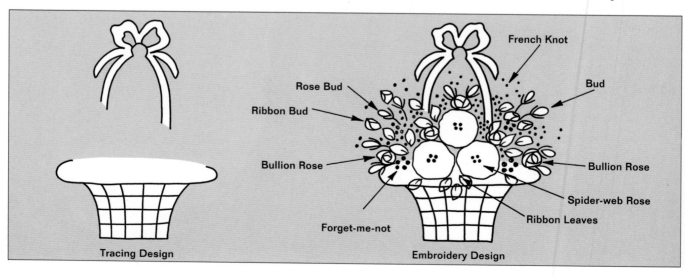

Tracing Design

Embroidery Design

French Knot
Rose Bud
Ribbon Bud
Bud
Bullion Rose
Bullion Rose
Spider-web Rose
Ribbon Leaves
Forget-me-not

TREASURED TIMES

Precious memories are preserved forever in this gracious design. Choose any photograph with special meaning and enhance it with embroidery.

MATERIALS

40 cm (16 in) square of cream homespun cotton
Crewel needle, size 10
Straw needle, size 10
Madeira Metallic Embroidery Thread, Gold
Sepia photograph or a coloured one, if you prefer (I used a 10 cm x 15 cm (4 in x 6 in) photograph)
Acid-free double-sided tape
Four brass corners
Stranded cotton:

DMC	Madeira
3726	810
3727	2610
225	0814
3740	2614
3041	0806
3042	0807
676	2208
677	2207
523	1512
524	1511
520	1514
932	1710
839	1913
310	Black
814	0514

Note: This piece has been worked in DMC Stranded Cotton.

PREPARATION

See the tracing and the embroidery designs on the Pull Out Pattern Sheet.

Trace the outline onto the fabric using the method described on page 79.

EMBROIDERY

Note: Embroider the flowers, following the Embroidery Guide on page 5 and the Stitch Guide on page 77. All the embroidery is worked in one strand unless stated otherwise.

STEP ONE

Embroider the Mauve pansies first. Using the crewel needle, embroider the back petal and the shading on the petal to the right of it in long and short satin stitches using 3740. Embroider the remainder of the shaded petal and the two side petals in 3041. Embroider the front petal in 3042. Using three or four buttonhole stitches, work the centre in 676. Embroider the face in Black long and short straight stitches. Finish with a French knot of two twists around the needle in 814 above the centre.

STEP TWO

Embroider the pink pansies in the same way as the Mauve one using the following threads: the back petal and shading in 3726, the remainder of the shaded petal and the two side petals in 3727, the front petal in 225.

STEP THREE

Using the crewel needle, embroider the leaves in long and short straight stitches in 523 and 524, using the darker colour on the top of the leaf. Place a straight stitch in 520 down the centre of the leaf.

STEP FOUR

Using the crewel needle, embroider the pansy buds, using 3041 for the back petal with 3042, and 3726 for the back petal with 3727.

STEP FIVE

Using the straw needle, embroider the bullion roses, beginning each rose with a 3 mm (³/₁₆ in) centre. Use 677 for the centre and 676 for the outer petals. Embroider the rose buds next in 677, then the rose leaves, using one bullion in 523. Finally, fill in with forget-me-nots in French knots of one twist around the needle in 932 with a French knot in the centre in 676. In some places you will only need to fill in with half flowers or just French knots. Don't try to have detailed flowers all through, just create an illusion of flowers – the French knots are sprinkled with no real flower form.

STEP SIX

Trace the words shown or write your own words, if you prefer. Embroider the writing in tiny straight stitches. I used Brown thread to blend with the sepia photograph.

MAKING UP

STEP ONE

Age the fabric by dyeing it in coffee, following the instructions on page 80.

STEP TWO

Completely cover the back of the photograph with the double-sided tape, then stick it into place on the fabric.

STEP THREE

Stitch on the brass corners with the metallic thread. If you are careful, you can stitch through the photographs themselves quite easily.

TREASURED TEDDY

A keepsake to treasure, this dear little teddy would make a wonderful gift for a special new baby.

Approximate size: 15 cm x 21 cm (6 in x 8 in)

MATERIALS

Two pieces of cream wool felt, each 20 cm x 34 cm (8 in x 13½ in)
Crewel needle, size 10
Straw needle, size 10
Two small brass heart charms
Button (old or new)
Polyester filling
Fine waterproof pen, Black
Felt-tipped pen, Black
Stranded cotton:

DMC	MADEIRA
310	Black
501	1704
502	1703
781	2213
839	1913
932	1710
3685	0602
3726	810
3727	2610
677	2207

Note: This piece has been worked in DMC Stranded Cotton.

PREPARATION

See the tracing and the embroidery designs on the Pull Out Pattern Sheet. You will only need to trace the front of the teddy.

STEP ONE

Trace the pattern, then tape it to a light box or a window on a sunny day. Trace the outline of the teddy with small dots (do not try to draw a solid line) with the waterproof pen (pencil will not be heavy enough). If the pattern tracing is not dark enough, go over the outline again with a black felt-tipped pen. This will enable you to see the design through the felt.

Note: The teddy is blanket-stitched around the edges to retain its lovely shape. Do not machine-sew. Felt shrinks when it is cut and shrinks a little more when it is filled, so the tracing appears much larger than the finished teddy.

STEP TWO

Trace the embroidery design lightly onto the front of the teddy.

EMBROIDERY

Note: Embroider the flowers and birds following the Embroidery Guide on page 5 and the Stitch Guide on page 77. All the embroidery is worked in one strand unless stated otherwise.

STEP ONE

Using the crewel needle, outline the eyes, mouth and nose with tiny back stitches in 839, then fill in the eyes and nose with satin stitches in the same colour.

STEP TWO

Outline the bow in tiny back stitches, then fill in with satin stitch. The top of the bow is 3685 and the bottom is 3726.

STEP THREE

Using the crewel needle and 932, embroider the birds in the heart garland in long and short satin stitches, overlapping the stitches to avoid a ridge forming. Using the straw needle and 310, work a French knot of one twist around the needle for the eye and two straight stitches in 781 for the beak.

STEP FOUR

Embroider the roses and leaves next, beginning them with a 3.5–4 mm (³/₁₆ in) bullion stitch centre. For the Pink roses, use 3726 for the centre and 3727 for the petals. For the Burgundy rose, use 3685 for the centre and 3726 for the petals. For each leaf, work one bullion in 501 and a second one close to it in 502. Keep the lighter shade to the top of the leaf. Fill in around the roses and leaves with tiny forget-me-nots in French knots of one twist around the needle in 932 with the centres in 781.

STEP FIVE

Using the crewel needle, embroider the bluebird and flowers on the left foot, as before. Work the branch in stem stitch in 501. Using the straw needle, work the buds in 3726 and the leaves in 501 in bullion stitches.

STEP SIX

Using the straw needle, embroider the design on the right leg, beginning with 3 mm (³/₁₆ in) bullion stitches for the rose buds in 3685 with a fly stitch around each one in 501. Extend the fly stitches to the centre of the posy, then work the bottom of the stems in stem stitch in 501 and 502.

STEP SEVEN

Using the crewel needle and 3685, embroider the tassel.

STEP EIGHT

Stitch the heart charms and the button into position. You may prefer to satin stitch the centre of the bow instead of using the button.

Note: For safety reasons, omit the buttons and charms if this is a baby's gift.

STEP NINE

Tie two bows, using the full six strands of 932, then stitch them in place with tiny stitches on the right foot and the left ear. Satin stitch over the top of the centre of the bows.

MAKING UP

STEP ONE

Place the two pieces of felt together with the wrong sides facing and baste them together 5 mm (¹/₄ in) inside the dotted line. Cut around just inside the dotted line with small scissors. Cut slowly and carefully to retain a nice rounded shape.

STEP TWO

Leave the basting in place and, using the crewel needle, commence blanket stitches in 677, starting at bottom and working up the left side. Try to keep the blanket stitches even and approximately 2 mm (¹/₈ in) apart. Work in blanket stitch until you reach the top of the left arm. Remove the basting only from the finished area. Commence filling the teddy in this area, then continue blanket stitching down the right side as far as the bottom of the right leg. Remove the basting in this area and fill the right arm and leg. Continue filling, keeping it even and making sure you get to the tips of the ears, hands and feet. Add or take out filling until you are happy with the shape. Do not make the teddy too fat, in case he bursts.

STEP THREE

Continue blanket stitching around the right leg up to approximately 2 cm (³/₄ in) from the beginning. Finish filling the right leg, then finish stitching the teddy closed.

For a very young child, omit the buttons and charms

ROSE COTTAGE

Paint and embroidery are perfectly combined to
create this charming cottage with its flowering garden.

Original sketch by Nic McLennan

MATERIALS

40 cm (16 in) square of cream
   homespun
Plaid Folk Art Acrylic Colours: Robins
   Nest, Plantation Green, Raspberry
   Sherbet, Amish Blue, Honeycomb,
   Buttercrunch
FolkArt Textile Medium
Francheville 200 pointed brush, size
   8 or 10
Waterproof pen
Stipple brush
Pencil, soft lead
Crewel needle, size 10
Straw needle, size 10
Stranded cotton:

DMC	Madeira
223	0812
225	0814
341	0901
501	1704
502	1703
503	1702
504	1701
3350	0603
3363	1602
3685	0602
3727	2610
550	0714
676	2208
677	2207
712	2101
743	0113
745	0111
778	0808
781	2213
814	0514
898	2006
932	1710
White	White

Note: This piece has been worked in
DMC Stranded Cotton.

PREPARATION

See the tracing and the embroidery
design on the Pull Out Pattern Sheet
and the painting guides for the cottage
on pages 42-43.

Trace the design onto the fabric using the method described on page 79.
Using the waterproof pen, draw over
the tracing.

PAINTING

STEP ONE

Note: I dilute my paints to watercolour
consistency before using them. However, it is still important to squeeze as
much water out of the brush as possible to stop the colours bleeding. It may
also help to use a hairdryer as you
paint. Follow the manufacturer's directions for using the textile medium .

Using Honeycomb, paint a wash
over the cottage. Using Amish Blue,
paint a wash on the roof and the chimney. Add a couple of strokes to the roof
in Buttercrunch. Using Amish Blue, with
the paint a little thicker, paint in the
fence and the tree trunk. Allow the
paint to dry.

The garden is a profusion of flowers

STEP TWO

Using Plantation Green, paint the veranda posts, roof spouting and window
frames. Using well-thinned Raspberry
Sherbet, paint in the door. Using Robins Nest, paint a wash over the garden.
Allow the paint to dry.

STEP THREE

Paint a very light wash of Amish Blue on
the windows. Using Plantation Green
and well-thinned Raspberry Sherbet,
paint the background for the plants on
the house and in the garden. Using
Plantation Green, outline a few edges
along the garden.

STEP FOUR

Using a stippling brush, stipple Amish
Blue and Raspberry Sherbet on the
tree, then stipple a little Robins Nest.

STEP FIVE

Heat-set the paints following the manufacturer's instructions.

EMBROIDERY

Note: Embroider the flowers following
the Embroidery Guide on page 5 and
the Stitch Guide on page 77. All the
embroidery is worked in one strand
unless stated otherwise.

STEP ONE

Using the pencil, lightly draw the outline of the rose bushes.

STEP TWO

Using the straw needle and 501, 502,
503 and White, embroider French
knots of one twist around the needle
on the left-hand side of the cottage
roof and the chimney.

STEP THREE

Using the straw needle, embroider the roses climbing up the side of the cottage, beginning each one with a bullion approximately 2 mm (¹/₈ in) long in 223 for the centre. Use 3727 for the outer petals.

STEP FOUR

Using the straw needle and 341, embroider small clusters of wisteria amongst the roses with French knots of one twist around the needle. Fill in around the roses and the wisteria with French knots in 501 and 502, intermingled with 712.

STEP FIVE

In the garden on the left-hand side of the cottage, using the straw needle, embroider French knots in 503, 504, 3727 and 712, varying from two twists around the needle at the bottom to one twist at the top (see 'Filler Flowers' on page 8). Embroider the same flowers on the other side of the cottage behind the fence and the gate.

STEP SIX

Using the pencil, lightly draw in the shape of the pink rose bush. Using the straw needle, embroider the roses, beginning each one with two 2 mm (¹/₈ in) bullion for the centre in 3727. In the same colour, embroider the two outer petals, meeting at a centre point at the bottom. Embroider the leaves around the outer edge of the flowers in single bullions in groups of three in 504. Using 504 and 503, fill in between the roses and leaves with French knots of one twist around the needle.

Using the crewel needle and 898, embroider the stem in two close rows of straight stitches. Make the stem a little crooked for a more realistic look.

Using the straw needle, 504 and 778, embroider a group of French knots of one twist around the needle under the bush.

STEP SEVEN

Using the pencil, lightly draw in the shape of the lemon rose bush. Using the straw needle and 676, begin embroidering the roses, beginning each with a 2.5 mm (¹/₈ in) long bullion for the centre. Embroider the outer petals in 677. Embroider the buds in 677 with a fly stitch surround in 503. Using the straw needle and 503, embroider the leaves as two bullions in groups of three. Using the straw needle, 503 and 504, fill in between the roses and leaves with French knots of one twist around the needle. Embroider the stem as for the pink rose bush.

Embroider a small clump of iris under the bush. Using the crewel needle and 504, embroider the leaves in straight stitches, then using 550, embroider the flowers in fly stitch with a lazy daisy stitch on top.

Using the straw needle and 743, work French knots of one twist around the needle and a few straight stitches in 503 under the irises.

To the left of the rose bush, at the base of the chimney, using the straw needle, embroider French knots of one twist around the needle in 932 and 712. Using the crewel needle and 503, work a few straight stitches under the French knots for the stems.

STEP EIGHT

Using the pencil, lightly draw in the shape of the red rose bush. Using the straw needle embroider the roses, beginning each with a 2.5 mm (¹/₈ in) long bullion in 814 for the centre. Embroider the outer petals in 3685 and the buds in the same colour with a fly stitch surround in 501. Using the straw needle and 501, embroider the leaves as two bullions in groups of three. Using the straw needle and 501, 502 and 504, fill in between the roses and leaves with French knots of one twist around the needle.

Work the stem in the same way as for the pink rose bush. Using the pencil, lightly draw in the shape of the lavender bush. Using the crewel needle and 504, embroider feather stitches over the outline. Using the straw needle and 341, work a bullion stitch, approximately 2 mm (¹/₈ in) long, at the tip of each feather stitch and in any spaces.

Using the crewel needle and 504, fill in around the flowers and around the edge of the bush with tiny straight stitches in any direction.

Next to the lavender, draw in the outline of the daisy bush. Using the crewel needle and 3363, embroider feather stitches over the outline. Using the crewel needle and 712, embroider the daisy petals (five for the full flower, three for the half flower and two for the bud). Using the straw needle and 781, work a French knot of one twist around the needle for the centres.

Using the crewel needle and 3363, fill in around the flowers and the edge of the bush with tiny straight stitches in any direction. Using the straw needle and 712, embroider a few French knots of one twist around the needle on the bush. Using the straw needle, 743 and 502, embroider French knots of one twist around the needle at the bottom of the daisy bush.

STEP NINE

Embroider lemon roses among the fence posts, placing a 3 mm (³/₁₆ in) bullion in 743 for the centre. Embroider the outer petals in 745 and the buds in 743 with a fly stitch surround in 503. Using the straw needle and 501, embroider the leaves with two bullions in groups of three. Where the leaves trail up the cottage and at the top of the fence, work tiny single bullion leaves in groups of three.

STEP TEN

Using the crewel needle and 501, embroider geranium leaves along the bottom of the fence. Embroider the flowers in 3350 (see page 5).

Using the crewel needle, 932 and 781, embroider a group of forget-me-nots with French knots of one twist around the needle. Work a row of tiny straight stitches under the French knots in 504. Embroider another clump of geraniums and another group of iris in 550 and 504. Using the straw needle, work small French knots of one twist around the needle under the irises in 743 and in 502.

STEP ELEVEN

Using the crewel needle and two strands of 712, embroider two foxgloves using upside-down lazy daisy stitches, starting with three stitches and reducing to one at the top. Using the straw needle and 712, work three French knots varying from two to one twist around the needle at the top. Work another lazy daisy stitch inside the ones already worked. Using the crewel needle and two strands of 502, embroider a few leaves for the base of the third flower. Work a straight stitch inside each lazy daisy stitch, then complete the flower using two strands of 712.

Embroider another clump of geraniums at the base of the foxgloves.

Using the straw needle, 743 and 3363, embroider a few French knots of one twist around the needle between the foxgloves and the hollyhocks.

STEP TWELVE

Sketch in the hollyhocks. Using the crewel needle and 502, embroider full circle leaves in buttonhole stitch. Using 501 and 502, embroider half leaves sitting under them. Using the crewel needle, 3685, 677 and 3727, work the flowers in full circles of buttonhole stitch. Using the straw needle, work two or three French knots, varying from two twists around the needle to one, at the top of the flowers. Using the straw needle, place a contrasting French knot in the centre of each flower, if you wish.

Using the crewel needle, 502 and 503, work straight stitch stems. At the bottom of the fence, work a few French knots of one twist around the needle in 743 and 3363. Embroider another clump of geraniums, then a few more French knots in 743 and 3363.

STEP THIRTEEN

Embroider the roses over the arch, placing a bullion 2 mm (¹/₈ in) long in 778 for the centre. Embroider the outer petals in 225. Note that some roses have only a few petals. Using the straw needle, fill in around the roses with French knots varying from one to two twists around the needle in 503 and 504. Work French knots up the right side of the arch in 503, 504 and 712.

STEP FOURTEEN

Using the crewel needle and two strands of 712, embroider small foxgloves as before. Using the crewel needle, 503 and 504, add a few French knots of one twist around the needle at the base of the foxgloves.

STEP FIFTEEN

Using the pencil, outline the tiny rose bush. Using the straw needle and 778, embroider the roses, placing a 2 mm (¹/₈ in) long bullion for the centre. Embroider the outer petals and the buds in 225, with a fly stitch in 503 around the buds. Using the straw needle and 504, embroider the leaves as single bullions in groups of three around the edge of the roses. Using the straw needle, 503 and 504, fill in around the roses with French knots of one twist around the needle. Embroider a small lavender bush at the base of the rose bush using bullion stitches in 341 at the top of straight stitches in 504.

Embroider another clump of geraniums as before. Using the crewel needle and 743, work a French knot of one twist around the needle on each side of the geraniums.

STEP SIXTEEN

Using the straw needle and 341, embroider small bunches of wisteria in French knots of one twist around the needle up the veranda posts and along the top of the front of the cottage. Using the crewel needle and 503, work French knots of one twist around the needle close to the wisteria flowers to give the impression of leaves.

Climbing roses and wisteria decorate the cottage roof

PEDESTAL AND URN

**A classic design executed in tiny embroidery stitches
makes this piece an heirloom for tomorrow.**

MATERIALS

30 cm (12 in) square of ivory home-
spun cotton
Crewel needle, size 10
Straw needle, size 10
Fine-tip waterproof pen
Plaid Folk Art Acrylic Paints: Amish
Blue, Buttercrunch, Plantation
Green, Robins Nest, Raspberry
Sherbet
FolkArt Textile Medium
Francheville pointed brush, size 8
or 10
Stranded Cotton:

DMC	MADEIRA
502	1703
503	1702
745	0111
932	1710
504	1701
316	0809
778	0808
3042	0807
781	2213

Note: This piece has been worked in
Madeira Stranded cotton.

PREPARATION

See the tracing and the embroidery
designs on page 46.

Trace the outline of the pedestal and
urn onto the fabric using the method
described on page 79.

PAINTING

STEP ONE

Using the waterproof pen, draw over
the outline of the pedestal and urn.

STEP TWO

Note: Apply the paints and textile
medium following the manufacturer's
directions for painting on fabric.
Using Amish Blue, paint a wash over
the pedestal and urn. Paint a wash of
Buttercrunch in the centre of the
pedestal and urn.

STEP THREE

Paint a soft wash around the outer
edge of the urn as shown in the painting guide on page 46. When the paint
is dry, paint around base of pedestal.

STEP FOUR

In the top left-hand corner, paint
'shadow' leaves with Robins Nest and
Raspberry Sherbet. Try to remove
most of the moisture from the brush
when doing this to prevent bleeding.

STEP FIVE

Heat-set the paints, following the
manufacturer's instructions.

EMBROIDERY

Note: Embroider the flowers following
the Embroidery Guide on page 5 and
the Stitch Guide on page 77. All the
embroidery is worked in one strand
unless stated otherwise.

STEP ONE

Using the straw needle, embroider the
main roses and leaves first, beginning
the rose with a bullion approximately
3 mm (³/₁₆ in) long. Use 0809 for the
centres, 0808 for the outer petals and
1703 for the leaves.

Fill all the spaces around the main flowers with forget-me-nots

45

STEP TWO

Using the straw needle and 0111, embroider the single roses in a circle of five French knots of three twists around the needle with a French knot in the centre in 2213. Embroider the rose buds in 0809 with a fly stitch surround in 1703.

Embroider the leaves in one bullion in 1701. Fill all through the design with forget-me-nots in French knots of one twist around the needle using 1710. For the forget-me-not centres, work a French knot in 2213.

STEP THREE

Using the crewel needle and 0807, embroider the wisteria, varying the number of twists around the needle from two to one. Using the crewel needle and 1702, embroider the wisteria leaves in tiny lazy daisy stitches.

Tracing Design   **Embroidery Design**

PETER'S CHOICE

For a long time, my husband Peter has wanted me
to embroider a burgundy rose on a black background.
This is the same rose as appears in Pink Ice.

MATERIALS

30 cm (12 in) square of black dupion
silk (Black dupion silk is quite
transparent when it has a light
behind it.)
Crewel needle, size 10
Straw needle, size 10
Embroidery hoop
Blue marker for tracing
Stranded cotton:

DMC	Madeira
500	1705
501	1704
781	2213
814	0514
931	1711
3685	0602

Note: This piece has been worked
in DMC Stranded Cotton.

PREPARATION

See the embroidery and the tracing
designs on the Pull Out Pattern Sheet.
   Trace the design onto the black silk
using the method described on page 79.

EMBROIDERY

Embroider the flowers following the
Embroidery Guide on page 5 and the
Stitch Guide on page 79. Use the embroidery hoop for the long and short
satin stitches but remove it when you
are not embroidering. All the embroidery is worked in one strand unless
stated otherwise.

STEP ONE

Using the crewel needle and 3685,
outline the rose in back stitch.

STEP TWO

Using the embroidery diagram as a
guide for the placement of the shading,
fill in the darker colour with long and
short satin stitches in 814, overlapping
the stitches to ensure that there are no
ridges. Refer to the embroidery diagram for the direction of these stitches.

STEP THREE

Using the crewel needle and 3685, fill
in the rest of the rose. The turnbacks
have a definite line so work these in
satin stitch in 3685.

STEP FOUR

Using the crewel needle and 501, outline the leaves in back stitch as for the
rose, then fill in the darker shade first
in 500, then the lighter shade in 501.

STEP FIVE

For the bud, embroider the inner centre in long and short straight stitches in
814 and the outer centre in 3685, then
work the outer parts in long and short
satin stitch in 500 and 501. Refer to the
embroidery diagram for the shading.

STEP SIX

Work the stem in stem stitch using 500
and 501.

STEP SEVEN

Using the straw needle, embroider the
forget-me-nots in French knots of two
twists using 931 for the petals and 781
for the centres.

The black background is the perfect foil for a red rose

PINK ICE

Capture a perfect single rose in embroidery.
The stitches used are quite simple, but the effect is stunning.

MATERIALS

30 cm (12 in) square of ivory dupion silk for the embroidery
25 cm (10 in) of ivory dupion silk for the ruffle
30 cm (12 in) of pink linen for the borders and pillow back
Crewel needle, size 10
Straw needle, size 10
Embroidery hoop
30 cm x 35 cm (12 in x 14 in) pillow insert
Four fancy buttons
Four purchased tassels
Stranded cotton:

DMC	Madeira
819	0501
225	0814
523	1512
524	1511
Ecru	Ecru
3364	1603

Note: This piece has been worked in DMC Stranded Cotton.

PREPARATION

See the tracing and the embroidery designs on the Pull Out Pattern Sheet.

Trace the design onto the silk using the method described on page 79.

EMBROIDERY

Note: Work the embroidery following the Stitch Guide on page 77. I recommend that you use the embroidery hoop when working the long and short satin stitches but remove it when you are not embroidering. All the embroidery is worked in one strand unless stated otherwise.

STEP ONE

Using the crewel needle, outline the rose in back stitch using 225.

STEP TWO

Using the embroidery diagram as a guide for the placement of the colours, fill in the darker shading in 819 with long and short satin stitches, overlapping them to ensure that there are no ridges. Refer to the embroidery diagram for the direction of these stitches.

STEP THREE

Using the crewel needle and 225, fill in the rest of the rose. The turnbacks have a definite line so work these in satin stitch in 225.

STEP FOUR

Using the crewel needle, outline the leaves in back stitch using 524 as for the rose, then fill in the darker shade first in 3364, then the medium shade in 523, then the lighter shade in 524.

STEP FIVE

For the bud, using the crewel needle, embroider the centre in 819 and 225 then work the outer parts in long and

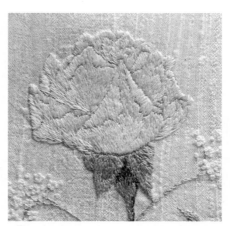
The shading on the rose is quite delicate

short satin stitches in 523 and 524. Add a few stitches in 3364 at the base.

STEP SIX

Work the stem in back stitch in 523, then whipstitch in 524.

STEP SEVEN

Using the straw needle, embroider clusters of French knots in Ecru, varying from three twists around the needle in the centre to two twists around the needle at the outer edge.

MAKING UP

STEP ONE

Cut two pieces of pink linen, each 7 cm x 17 cm (2³/₄ in x 8 in), and two pieces, each 7 cm x 35 cm (2³/₄ in x 14 in). Cut one piece of pink linen 30 cm x 35 cm (12 in x 14 in) for the pillow back. Sew the smaller pieces to the top and bottom of the embroidered piece, and the longer pieces to the sides.

STEP TWO

Finish the pillow in the same way as the May Sunshine pillow on page 14, sewing the ruffles 6 cm (2³/₈ in) wide (doubled) and mitring the corners as shown in the photograph.

STEP THREE

In each corner of the pillow, stitch a tassel with a button over the top. Catch the tassel down along the mitre with a few tiny stitches.

CHRISTMAS TREE

A beautiful Christmas tree is the centre of family celebrations. Embroider your own tree, complete with tinsels, baubles and star.

MATERIALS

30 cm (12 in) square of cream homespun cotton
Crewel needle, size 10
Straw needle, size 10
Mill Hill small glass beads: Burgundy, Blue, Antique Gold
Madeira Metallic Embroidery Thread, Gold 3004
Brass charms (optional)
Embroidery hoop
Stranded Cotton:

DMC	MADEIRA
3362	1601
550	0714
781	2213
500	1705
898	2006

Note: This piece has been worked in Madeira Stranded Cotton.

PREPARATION

See the embroidery and the tracing designs on this page. Trace the design onto the fabric, using the method described on page 79.

EMBROIDERY

Note: For the embroidery, follow the Stitch Guide on page 77. All the embroidery is worked in one strand unless stated otherwise.

STEP ONE

Using the crewel needle and 1705, embroider the tree in long and short satin stitches, beginning at the top and working down. Refer to the design below for the slope of the stitches.

STEP TWO

Using the crewel needle, embroider the presents under the tree in satin stitch, using the photograph as a guide for the colours. Satin stitch the ribbons around the parcels in 3004.

STEP THREE

Using the crewel needle, satin stitch the trunk of the tree in 2006.
Using the straw needle and 0714, 0601 and 3004, place a small French knot of one twist around the needle on the tip of each branch.

STEP FOUR

Using the crewel needle and 3004, back stitch the tinsel lines down the tree. Sew on the beads all over the tree, securing each bead with one or two stitches on the back. Place some more beads at the bottom of the tree and among the presents.
Note: If you wish to age the piece by dyeing with tea or coffee, do it now before the charms are attached.

STEP FIVE

Sew on the charms with the metallic thread. If you can't find a suitable star charm for the tree top, embroider one in 2213 with a double cross stitch.

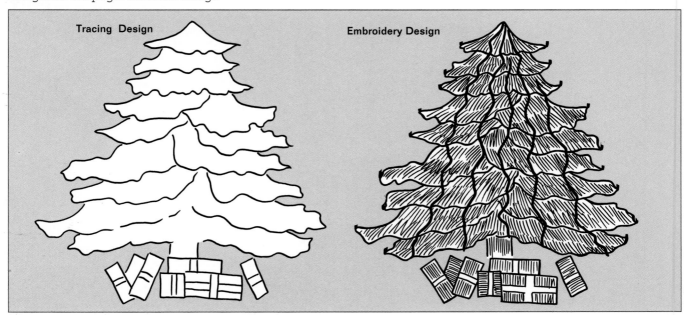

Tracing Design

Embroidery Design

Toy soldiers from Peter Nathan Collectables, Woollahra NSW

ROSE AND WISTERIA GARLAND

This delightful embroidered garland perfectly complements the
pretty country look of the pillow.

MATERIALS

30 cm (12 in) square of homespun
  for the embroidery
Crewel needle, size 10
Straw needle, size 10
15 cm (6 in) of checked cotton fabric
60 cm (24 in) of purple cotton fabric
  for the pillow back and ruffle
Embroidery hoop
Madeira Stranded Cotton:
  0810
  0601
  0806
  1702
  2105
  Ecru
  2213
  1710
  1701
Four wooden buttons
25 cm (10 in) square pillow insert

PREPARATION

See the tracing and the embroidery
designs on this page.

Trace the design onto the fabric using the method described on page 79.

EMBROIDERY

Note: Embroider the flowers following
the Embroidery Guide on page 5 and
the Stitch Guide on page 77. All the
embroidery is worked in one strand
unless stated otherwise.

STEP ONE

Using the crewel needle and 0601 and
the embroidery hoop, work the bow in
satin stitch.

STEP TWO

Using the straw needle, embroider all
the roses and buds, using 0601 for the
centres and 0810 for the outer petals.
Begin each rose with a bullion approximately 4 mm (³/₁₆ in) long.

STEP THREE

Using the straw needle and 1702, embroider the rose leaves in bullion
stitch, placed as shown.

STEP FOUR

Using the straw needle and 0806, embroider the wisteria blossoms and,
with the same colour, fill in the areas
shown with French knots for an illusion of wisteria, varying the twists
around the needle from three at the
top to two, then to one at the bottom.

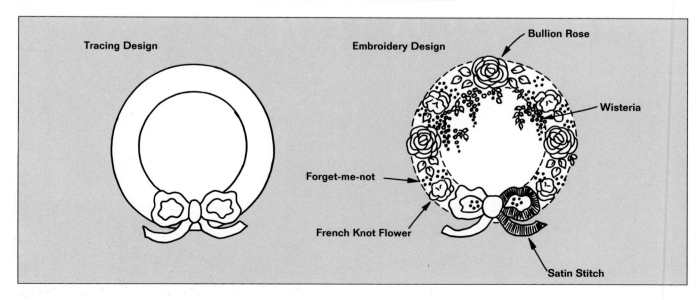

STEP FIVE

Using the straw needle and Ecru, embroider the French knot flowers with two twists around the needle. Work a French knot in 2213 for the centre.

STEP SIX

Using the straw needle and 1710, embroider the forget-me-nots in French knots of one twist around the needle throughout the rest of the design. Work a French knot in 2213 for the centres.

STEP SEVEN

Using the crewel needle and 1701, embroider tiny lazy daisy leaves on the inner circle. Fill in the remaining gaps in French knots in 0806 and 1702. Embroider the curled stems in tiny back stitches, using 2105.

Note: If you wish to age your piece, dye it in coffee or tea as instructed on page 80.

MAKING UP

STEP ONE

Cut two pieces of checked fabric, each 7.5 cm x 13 cm (3 in x 5¼ in) and two pieces, each 7.5 cm x 24 cm (3 in x 9¾ in). Sew the smaller pieces to the top and bottom of the embroidered piece, then sew the other two pieces to the sides.

STEP TWO

Complete the pillow in the same way as the May Sunshine pillow on page 14, sewing the ruffle 7.5 cm (3 in) wide (doubled) and mitring the corners as shown in the photograph.

STEP THREE

Sew the four wooden buttons to the corners of the pillow, using burgundy-coloured thread.

This piece looks equally delightful framed

SHIRLEY'S GARDEN

This picture of a crinolined lady enjoying her garden is a real charmer.

MATERIALS

40 cm (16 in) square of crewel linen
Crewel needle, size 10
Straw needle, size 10
Madeira Silk Embroidery Floss:
  2209, 2401
Stranded Cotton:

DMC	MADEIRA
Ecru	Ecru
503	1702
502	1703
3052	1509
775	1001
932	1710
315	0810
316	0809
778	0808
3042	0807
3041	0806
414	1801
3023	1902
3046	2206
677	2207
422	2102
White	White

Note: This piece has been worked in Madeira Stranded Cotton.

PREPARATION

See the tracing and the embroidery designs on the Pull Out Pattern Sheet.

Trace the design onto the centre of the linen square using the method described on page 79. Also trace the rectangle which frames the design.

EMBROIDERY

Note: Embroider the flowers following the Embroidery Guide on page 5 and the Stitch Guide on page 77. All the embroidery is worked in one strand unless stated otherwise.

STEP ONE

Outline the dress and bonnet in 1710, using stem stitch. Fill in the bow with long and short satin stitches in 1710 and 1001, using the darker one for shading, as indicated on the diagram. Work the frill on the sleeve in 1001 and the shade on the bonnet in 1001 in buttonhole stitch. Using Ecru, work tiny circles of buttonhole stitch all over the skirt. Fill in the sleeve and the bonnet with tiny French knots of two twists around the needle in Ecru. Work half-circles in buttonhole stitch in the darker Blue around the bottom of the dress. Using the crewel needle and 2102, stitch the lady's hair in tiny straight stitches.

STEP TWO

For the basket, work satin stitches in a basketweave pattern, using the two shades of Gold silk. Work two rows of stem stitch in the lighter colour along the bottom of the basket.

STEP THREE

Using the photograph as a guide, embroider the flowers in the basket. Work the main roses first, then fill in with the remaining flowers. Using the straw needle and 0809, embroider the centres of the Pink roses, placing a 2½– 3 mm (³/₁₆ in) long bullion for the centre. Use 0808 for the outer petals.

Embroider the leaves in 1702.

Work the Burgundy roses in the

Fill the basket with masses of beautiful flowers

57

same way, using 0810 for the centres and 0809 for the outer petals. Embroider the leaves in 1703.

Using the crewel needle and Ecru, work the single roses in French knots of three twists around the needle. Work a French knot in the centre of the rose in 2206.

Using the straw needle and 0806, embroider the lavender flowers. Place a straight stitch in 1702 in between the flowers.

Fill in around the edge and in any bare spots with French knots of one twist around the needle in 1710.

STEP FOUR

Using the photograph as a guide, embroider the flowers in the garden beginning with the wisteria. Using the straw needle and 0806 and 1801, work French knots for the blossoms with three twists around the needle at the top of the flower, reducing to one twist around the needle towards the bottom. Using the straw needle and 1702, embroider the leaves using lazy daisy stitches in groups of five, seven or nine. Work the stems in small straight stitches using 1702.

STEP FIVE

Using the crewel needle, embroider the hollyhock flowers in circles of buttonhole stitch in 0810, 0809 and 0808. Next, work the leaves in the same stitch in 1702 and 1703. Use 1703 for the leaves tucked under the top ones. You will only need half leaves in some places. Work the stems in stem stitch.

Using the straw needle and 1710, 2206 and 1702, fill in the garden bed at the bottom of the hollyhocks with French knots of two twists around the needle in Blue, Yellow and Green to create the illusion of forget-me-nots.

STEP SIX

Using the crewel needle and 1509, outline the shape of the daisy bush in feather stitch. Using the crewel needle and two strands of White, embroider small daisy flowers over the bush. Using the straw needle and 2206, work French knots of two twists around the

needle for the daisy centres. Using the crewel needle and 1509, fill in around the flowers with tiny straight stitches in any direction. Place more straight stitches around the outer edge of the bush to create the illusion of leaves.

STEP SEVEN

Using the crewel needle and 2102, outline the rose bush in back stitches. Using the straw needle embroider the roses, placing a 2.5-3 mm ($^1/_8$-$^3/_{16}$ in) long bullion for the centre of each rose. Work the centres in 2206 and the outer petals in 2207. Using the straw needle and 1703, work the leaves in bullion stitch, using two bullions per leaf in groups of three. Using the straw needle, 1702 and 1703, work French knots of one and two twists around the needle throughout the bush. Using the crewel needle and 2102, embroider the tiny stems and branches in tiny back stitches.

STEP EIGHT

Using the crewel needle and 1702, outline the lavender bush in feather stitch. Using the straw needle and 0807, place a 3 mm ($^3/_{16}$ in) long bullion at the tip of each feather stitch and anywhere else there is room. Using the crewel needle and 1702, fill in around the lavender flowers and around the edge of the bush with tiny straight stitches in any direction.

STEP NINE

Using the straw needle and 2206 and 1702, work a border of French knots along the bottom right-hand edge to give the illusion of forget-me-nots.

STEP TEN

Along the top of the garden wall, using the straw needle, work French knots of two twists around the needle at the top, reducing to one twist lower down. Use 1702, 1703 and 1509.

STEP ELEVEN

Using the crewel needle and two strands of 1509, work the foxgloves in the garden and peeping over the gar-

den wall in five upside-down lazy daisy stitches. Place a straight stitch inside each one. Work another row the same. Change to two strands of 0809 and continue to work rows of lazy daisy stitches – approximately three rows of three, then two rows of two, then one row of one. Using the straw needle, work two or three French knots at the top of the flower, using two then one twist around the needle.

Using 0808 and 1509, embroider a foxglove on either side of the centre one. Using 0808, 0809 and 2207, embroider the tops of foxgloves peeping over the fence.

STEP TWELVE

Work the steps in stem stitch in 1902. Work the shading on the stair risers in straight stitches in the same shade. Work the horizontal shading on the steps in 1901.

MAKING UP

Have the picture professionally framed, taking care to place the mount as close as possible to the edge of the embroidery for the best effect.

CHRISTMAS IS FOR GIVING

A Christmas gift that keeps on giving year after year,
this embroidered picture is sure to be treasured by the recipient.

MATERIALS

35 cm (14 in) square of homespun
    cotton
Crewel needle, size 10
Straw needle, size 10
Small button
Small heart charm
Madeira Metallic Embroidery
    Thread, 3004
Stranded Cotton:

DMC	MADEIRA
502	1703
3045	2103
White	White
781	2213
3362	0601
315	0810
902	1601
550	0714

Note: This piece has been worked in
Madeira Stranded Cotton.

PREPARATION

See the tracing and the embroidery
designs on the Pull Out Pattern Sheet.
    Trace the outline and the embroi-
dery design, using the method described on page 79.

EMBROIDERY

Note: Embroider the flowers and tassels following the Embroidery Guide
on page 5 and the Stitch Guide on
page 77. All the embroidery is worked
in one strand unless stated otherwise.

STEP ONE

Using the crewel needle and 2103,
back stitch around the bow. Satin stitch
the bow in 2103, then satin stitch the
inside of the bow in 2213.

STEP TWO

Using the straw needle, embroider the
roses on the swag, using 0601 for the
centres and 0810 for the outer petals.
Embroider the leaves as six bullions in
three sets of two each in 1703. Fill in
around the roses and leaves with tiny
French knot flowers in 2103. These are
five French knots of two twists around
the needle in a close circle with a
French knot in 1703 in the centre.

STEP THREE

Using the straw needle, embroider the
roses and leaves around the heart and
fill in with tiny French knot flowers.

STEP FOUR

Link the heart to the bow with tiny
chain stitches in 2103; link the stockings to the swag in the same way.

STEP FIVE

Using the crewel needle, outline the
stockings in tiny back stitches in 0601.
The stocking on the right has a top
embroidered with French knots of two
twists around the needle in White, using the straw needle. The stocking on
the left has a satin stitch top in 0601,
using the crewel needle.

Highlight the bow with a special button

STEP SIX

Embroider the patterns on the stockings, following the embroidery diagram and key.

STEP SEVEN

Using the crewel needle, embroider
the tassels at the bottom of the heart
and the ends of the swag in 2103.

STEP EIGHT

Using the crewel needle and 0601,
embroider the motto using tiny back
stitches. I encourage you to use your
own writing for the motto. It took me
some time to be confident doing this,
but it makes the finished piece so
much more personal.

MAKING UP

STEP ONE

To age the piece and reduce the
brightness of the fabric and the embroidery, dye it in coffee, following the
instructions on page 80.

STEP TWO

Using the crewel needle and the metallic thread, carefully attach the button
in the centre of the bow and the heart
charm in the centre of the embroidered heart.

VIOLETS

Violets are the flowers of affection and are much
loved for their delicate beauty.

MATERIALS

25 cm (10 in) square of coffee
  dupion silk
Crewel needle, size 10
Straw needle, size 10
Embroidery hoop
Stranded Cotton:

DMC	MADEIRA
602	1702
603	1701
3041	0806
3042	0807
3046	2206
781	2213
932	1710
775	1001

Note: This piece has been worked in
  Madeira Stranded Cotton.

PREPARATION

See the tracing and the embroidery
designs on this page.

  Trace the design onto the centre of
the fabric using the method described
on page 79.

EMBROIDERY

Note: Embroider the flowers following
the Embroidery Guide on page 5 and
the Stitch Guide on page 77. All the embroidery is worked in one strand unless stated otherwise.

STEP ONE

Using the crewel needle, embroider
the ribbons in satin stitch using 1710
and 1001, placing the 1710 closer to
the violets for shading.

Work the violets over the bow

STEP TWO

Using the crewel needle and 1702, begin filling in the centre and tops of the
leaves in long and short satin stitches.
Complete the leaves in 1701. Embroider the stems in stem stitch, using 1701
and 1702.

STEP THREE

Using the crewel needle and 0806 and
0807, embroider the three main violets
in straight stitches of varying lengths.
Using 2213, work a French knot of two
twists around the needle in the centre.

  Using 0806, embroider the buds in
satin stitch with two tiny lazy daisy
stitches in 1702 at the top of the bud.
Embroider the stems in stem stitch
using 1702 and 1701.

STEP FOUR

Using the straw needle and 2206, embroider French knot flowers of three
twists around the needle throughout.
Work a French knot centre in 2213.

  Using the straw needle and 1710,
work some forget-me-nots. Work lazy
daisy stitch leaves in 1701.

Tracing Design

Bud

Violet

Lazy Daisy Stitch Leaf

Embroidery Design

PANSIES AND ROSES

Two all-time favourite flowers are combined in this miniature.

MATERIALS

25 cm (10 in) square of cream
    dupion silk
Crewel needle, size 10
Chenille needle, size 22
Straw needle, size 10
3 m (3¼ yd) of YLI silk ribbon:
    Medium Green, Fawn
Madeira Stranded Cotton:
    0810
    1511
    1509
    2105
    2204
    2103
    2006
    2206
    2213
    Ecru

PREPARATION

See the tracing and the embroidery
designs on this page.

    Trace the design onto the fabric us-
ing the method described on page 79.

EMBROIDERY

Embroider the flowers following the
Embroidery Guide on page 5 and the
Stitch Guide on page 77. All the embroidery is worked in one strand unless stated otherwise.

STEP ONE

Using the crewel needle, embroider
the outline of the bowl in small back
stitches using 2105. Work the pattern
on the vase in back stitch.

STEP TWO

Using the crewel needle, embroider
the pansies in the following colours:
• For the two back pansies, work the
back petal in 2105, the petal opposite
in 2103, the next two petals in 2204 and
the front petal in 2206. Embroider the
face in 2006 and work the French knot
in the centre in 2213.
• For the two side pansies, embroider
the side petals in 2105 and the front
petal in 2103. Embroider the face in
0810 and work the French knot in the
centre in 2213.
• For the centre pansy, embroider the
side petals in 2204 and the front petal
in 2206. Embroider the face in 2006
and the French knot centre in 2213.
    Embroider the buds in buttonhole
stitch, using the picture as a guide.

STEP THREE

Using the crewel needle, embroider
the leaves in long and short satin stitch
using 1511 at the tip and 1509 at the
top. Embroider the stems in stem stitch
in 1509.

STEP FOUR

Mark the positions of the spider-web
roses. Using the chenille needle, work
them next in Fawn, following the stitch
guide. Work the silk ribbon leaves in
Medium Green, then the buds in ribbon stitch, as well. Work a fly stitch in
1509 around the buds.

STEP FIVE

Using the straw needle and Ecru, work
the French knot flowers around the
pansies, using three twists around the
needle. Work a French knot for the
centres in 2213. Finish by embroidering tiny lazy daisy leaves around the
outside of the design, using the crewel
needle and 1511.

Tracing Design

Embroidery Design

Spider-web roses in silk ribbon

TEDDY OF HEARTS

Tired of baby blue and baby pink. Then this richly coloured baby's blanket may be the perfect alternative.

MATERIALS

60 cm x 84 cm (24 in x 33 in) piece of wool blanket or flannel

1 m (1¹/₃ yd) of cotton print fabric for the backing

Two pieces of cream wool felt, each 20 cm x 32 cm (8 in x 13 in)

50 cm (20 in) of double-sided cream satin ribbon

Small bow and heart charms

Crewel needles, sizes 8 and 10

Straw needles, sizes 8 and 10

Waterproof pen, Black

Felt-tipped pen, Black

Tailor's pencil

Small scissors

Metallic Madeira Embroidery Thread, Gold

Ordinary sewing thread

Stranded cottons:

DMC	Madeira
225	0814
341	0901
503	1702
504	1701
677	2207
738	2013
781	2213
932	1710
3041	0806
3042	0807
3727	2610
3740	2614
Ecru	Ecru

Note: This piece has been worked in DMC Stranded Cotton.

PREPARATION

See the tracing and the embroidery designs on the Pull Out Pattern Sheet.

Transfer the teddy outline onto the felt with small dots (do not try to draw a solid line) using the waterproof pen (pencil will not be heavy enough). If the pattern tracing is not dark enough, go over the outline again with a black felt-tipped pen. This will enable you to see the design through the fabric.

TEDDY EMBROIDERY

Note: Embroider the flowers following the Embroidery Guide on page 5 and the Stitch Guide on page 77. All the embroidery is worked in one strand unless stated otherwise.

STEP ONE

Using the size 10 crewel needle, outline the eyes with back stitches in 3042, then fill in with satin stitches in the same colour. Work the nose in the same way using 738. Embroider the mouth in tiny back stitches in 3042.

STEP TWO

Using the size 10 straw needle, embroider the pink rose on the right ear using 3727 for the centre and 225 for the outer petals. Begin with a bullion approximately 3 mm (³/₁₆ in) long. For the cream rose, use 677 for the centre and Ecru for the outer petals. Begin with a bullion approximately 3 mm (³/₁₆ in) long. Work three French knots of one twist around the needle between the roses and a little lavender in 341 at the base of the lemon rose.

STEP THREE

Using the size 10 crewel needle and 503, work feather stitch around both heart outlines. On the tip of each feather stitch on the inner heart, using the size 10 straw needle, work a French knot flower of two twists around the needle in 3740. Using 3727, work French knot flowers around the hearts, in between the purple ones. Work a French knot of two twists around the needle in the centres using 677.

STEP FOUR

Using the size 10 straw needle, embroider the roses around the larger heart, using the same threads as for the roses on the ear. Begin with a bullion approximately 3 mm (³/₁₆ in) long. Using 341, work lavender to fill in between the roses. Work straight stitches in 504 between the lavender bullions. Embroider the tassel in 3041.

STEP FIVE

Using the size 10 crewel needle and 3740, embroider in chain stitch around the upper heart on the left leg. Using 3042 and stem stitch, work around the lower heart, then embroider the roses in the same way as for the ear. Tie a small six-strand bow and stitch it in place above the chain stitch heart with a French knot centre.

STEP SIX

Using the size 10 crewel needle and 504, embroider two lines of feather stitch on the right leg. Using the size 10 straw needle, embroider a bullion in 341 at the tip of each feather stitch and fill in with tiny straight stitches in 504. Embroider the stems in stem stitch.

STEP SEVEN

Using the metallic thread, sew on the bow and heart charms. Tie a small six-strand bow in 3727 and stitch it onto the lavender spray. Tie another one in 3041 and stitch it onto the left ear. Tie a satin bow and stitch it under the chin. **Note:** For safety reasons, you may prefer to omit the charms.

BLANKET

STEP ONE

Using a small pair of scissors, cut out the teddy very carefully. Pin, then blanket stitch it onto the blanket, filling it lightly as you go. Do not overfill and try to keep the blanket stitches as even as possible.

STEP TWO

Using the tailor's pencil, sketch the skipping rope onto the blanket or embroider it freehand, if you prefer. Using the size 8 crewel needle, outline the skipping rope in feather stitch in two strands of 503. Using the size 8 crewel needle, embroider the daisies in two strands of 677 with a French knot centre in 781.

STEP THREE

Using the size 8 straw needle, embroider the pink roses in the same shades as on the teddy, but using three strands of thread. Begin with a bullion approximately 6 mm ($^1/_4$ in) long.

STEP FOUR

Using the size 8 straw needle and 932, fill in around the flowers on the skipping rope with forget-me-nots using French knots of two twists around the needle with a French knot in 781 for the centre.

STEP FIVE

Using the size 8 crewel needle, embroider the tassels for the skipping rope handles using 3042.

MAKING UP

STEP ONE

Lay the backing fabric face down with the wool blanket on top, face upwards. Make sure the blanket is centred on the backing and that both are smooth and flat. Baste them together from the centre to the corners and to all four sides.

STEP TWO

Trim the backing so that it is 7 cm ($2^3/_4$ in) bigger than the wool blanket. Baste around the wool blanket 2.5 cm (1 in) from the edge. This is the guide for the border.

Fold the backing to the edge of the wool blanket, then fold it again to the basted guide. Pin the border in place on the blanket. Fold the mitres at the corners and pin those as well. Stitch the border down onto the blanket by hand or by machine. At the corners, slipstitch the mitres into place.

The purple wool flannel is available from the Fancyworks stand at major needlework and craft shows.

For a young baby, replace the charm with an embroidered bow

WEDDING MEMORIES

Wedding memorabilia are always treasured and yet are so
often locked away in a dusty album. Here is a delightful
way to preserve them and have them available to be enjoyed.

MATERIALS

60 cm (22 in) square of backing
   fabric, such as damask, silk or
   furnishing fabric
Pieces of lace, old or new
Motifs for the corners
Brass corner for photo
Buttons, charms, pieces of jewellery
   (old or new)
Two photographs, approximately
   15 cm x 20 cm (6 in x 8 in) and
   10 cm x 15 cm (4 in x 6 in)
2 m (2¼ yd) of silk ribbon, Coffee
   (for the frame)
Template plastic
Small piece of cardboard
Acid-free double-sided tape
Small pearls
18 cm (7 in) square of cream home-
   spun for the name plaque
1 m (1⅛ yd) of 7 mm (⁵⁄₁₆ in) wide YLI
   silk ribbon: Dark Green, Camel
1.5 m (1⅔ yd) of 7 mm (⁵⁄₁₆ in) wide
   YLI silk ribbon: Cream, Light Brown
1 m (1⅓ yd) of 3 mm (³⁄₁₆ in) wide YLI
   silk ribbon, Dusty Pink
Straw needle, size 10
Crewel needle, size 10
Chenille needle, size 26
Pencil
Stranded cotton:

DMC	MADEIRA
3362	1601
869	2105
316	0809
315	0810
3052	1509

Note: This piece has been worked in
Madeira Stranded Cotton.

PREPARATION

See the template on page 70.

Pencil the outline of the photographs onto the background fabric.
Stitch the lace pieces around these
marked edges with fine stitches, making sure you catch the edges securely.
Use a different lace on each side of the
outline.

EMBROIDERY

Note: Embroider the flowers following
the Embroidery Guide on page 5 and
the Stitch Guide on page 77. All the
embroidery is worked in one strand
unless stated otherwise.

STEP ONE

In the top left-hand corner and using
the chenille needle, embroider the
ribbon roses, working the five larger
spider-web roses first. Next, work the
stem stitch roses in Dusty Pink and
the ribbon stitch daisies and buds
in Cream. Sew a pearl in the centre
of each daisy. Work a fly stitch around the ribbon bud in 1601 and the
leaves in ribbon stitch in Dark Green.
Stitch a large lace motif in the right-
hand corner.

Embroider the names and date for a permanent record

Using the double-sided tape, completely cover the back of the larger photograph and stick it into position. Do the same with the smaller photograph. Stitch a length of lace over the left-hand edge and the top of the larger photograph. I used a little double-sided tape under the lace that sits on the photograph, and stitched down the lace over the background fabric.

STEP THREE

Stick the horseshoe or some other wedding memento into position over the bottom left-hand corner. I used acid-free double-sided tape to attach it over the photograph, then stitched the ribbon down. Stitch the tassel and the corner motifs into position.

STEP FOUR

Lightly trace the outline of the inner frame onto the homespun fabric. Lightly write the names and date in the centre of the homespun and embroider them with tiny backstitches in 2105. Using the straw needle, embroider the rose centres in 0810 and the petals in 0809. Embroider the rose buds in 0810 and place a fly stitch around it in 1509. Embroider a single bullion for the leaves in 1509.

STEP FIVE

Cut a cardboard template and centre the embroidered piece on it, then glue the edges onto the back.

STEP SIX

Trace both outlines of the frame onto the template plastic. With nail scissors, cut around the outline. To achieve a smooth edge, keep your hand and the scissors still and move the plastic around. Glue the end of the ribbon to the plastic, then wind the ribbon around the frame, gluing the other end down again at the finish. Using the acid-free, double-sided tape, stick the embroidered plaque to the corner of the photograph, then attach the frame over the top. Glue on a brooch, button or charm at the top.

STEP SEVEN

Embroider the large ribbon rose in Cream and the leaves in Dark Green silk ribbon in the upper right-hand corner. Stick the framed plaque in place with the acid-free double-sided tape.

STEP EIGHT

Stitch the heart charms and the button at the top of the horseshoe ribbon. Stitch on any other keepsakes, as desired. Stitch the brass photo corner into position or glue it. Attach the card with the double-sided tape.

MAKING UP

To protect your piece, have it professionally framed as shown here, or in a box frame for extra depth.

Antiqued laces are available from Judith and Kathryn Design stands at major needlework and craft shows.

Make ribbon roses with delicate silk ribbon

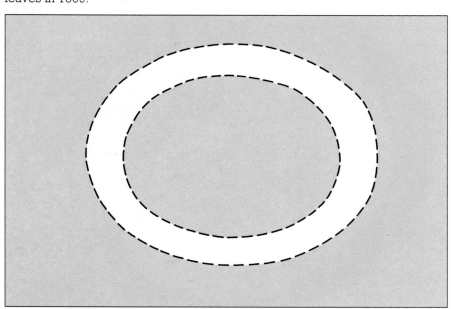

Template

SACRED CROSS

Ecclesiastical embroidery has a wonderful history.
This piece is an unusual variation on the traditional technique
as it uses tiny roses to define the cross.

MATERIALS

30 cm (12 in) square of antique gold
  dupion silk
Crewel needle, size 10
Straw needle, size 10
Madeira Silk Embroidery Floss, Black
Madeira Metallic Embroidery
  Thread, Gold
Stranded Cotton:

DMC	MADEIRA
315	0810
902	0601
3052	1509
3041	0806
781	2213
Ecru	Ecru
932	1710

Note: This piece has been stitched in
Madeira Stranded Cotton.

PREPARATION

See the tracing and the embroidery
designs on this page.

  Trace the outline of the cross onto
the centre of the fabric, using the
method described on page 79.

EMBROIDERY

Note: Embroider the flowers following
the Embroidery Guide on page 5 and
the Stitch Guide on page 77. All the
embroidery is worked in one strand
unless stated otherwise.

STEP ONE

Using the crewel needle, commence
embroidering around the outer edge
of the cross, using the Black silk thread
and back stitch. Work around inner
and outer edges of border in this way.
When the outline is completed, fill in
the border with satin stitches in Black
silk thread.

STEP TWO

Using the straw needle, embroider the
main roses and leaves first. For the
bullion roses, begin with a bullion
stitch approximately 3–3.5 mm ($^3/_{16}$ in)
long for the centre of the rose. Work
the centres in 0601, the petals in 0810
and the leaves in 1509.

STEP THREE

Using the straw needle, embroider the
Ecru single roses in French knots of
three twists around the needle. Work a
French knot of two twists around the
needle in Black silk for the centre.

STEP FOUR

Using the straw needle, embroider
forget-me-nots in French knots in 1710
through the design, then add more
French knots in 0806 and 0810. Work
French knots in the centres of the forget-me-nots in 2213. All these French
knots have two twists around the
needle. Keep filling in with French
knots until there are no bare spots.

STEP FIVE

Using the crewel needle and one
strand of metallic thread, outline the
outer and inner edge of the border in
back stitch.

STEP SIX

Trim the embroidery to the shape and
size you prefer. The rectangle shape
shown here complements the shape of
the cross very well.

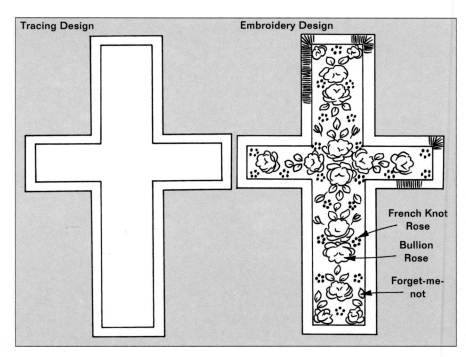

Tracing Design   Embroidery Design

French Knot Rose

Bullion Rose

Forget-me-not

FORGET-ME-NOT

**Let a special friend know how much they
mean to you with this embroidered keepsake.**

MATERIALS

45 cm (18 in) square of linen
Crewel needle, size 10
Straw needle, size 10
Purchased tassel
Special button
Brooch or charm
15 cm (6 in) square of template
   plastic
2.5 m (2³/₄ yd) of narrow satin ribbon
Acid-free double-sided tape
Craft glue
Embroidery hoop
Photo (a black-and-white or sepia
   photograph is usually preferable)
Stranded Cotton:

DMC	MADEIRA
932	1710
729	2209
503	1702
902	0601
318	1802
315	0810
677	2207
502	1703
404	1801

Note: This piece has been worked in
Madeira Stranded Cotton.

PREPARATION

See the tracing and the embroidery
designs on page 76. Use the template
on page 70.

Trace the outline onto the fabric, using the method described on page 79.

EMBROIDERY

Note: Embroider the flowers following
the Embroidery Guide on page 5 and
the Stitch Guide on page 77.

All the embroidery is worked in one
strand unless stated otherwise.

STEP ONE

Using the crewel needle and 1710,
embroider the outline of the envelope
in stem stitch. Work half buttonhole
stitches around the edge of the note-
paper, beginning at one corner so
there is a nice, round edge. To ensure
a round edge at the other corner, you
may have to go a little higher than the
traced line.

STEP TWO

Using the crewel needle and 1801,
embroider the writing in tiny back
stitches.

STEP THREE

For the bouquet, using the straw needle, embroider the main flowers first.
For the centre of the rose, begin with a
bullion stitch approximately 4 mm
(³/₁₆ in) long. Work the centres in 0601
and the outer petals in 0810.

STEP FOUR

Using the straw needle and 2207, work
the single roses in French knots of
three twists around the needle with a
French knot centre in 2209. Using the
straw needle, work the buds in 0601
with a fly stitch surround in 1703.

STEP FIVE

Finally, using the straw needle and
1710, fill in with forget-me-nots in
French knots of two twists around the
needle with a French knot of two twists
around the needle in 2207 in the centre. Place forget-me-not buds in the
same colour around the outer edge,
reducing from two twists around the
needle to one. Work the stems in stem
stitch in 1702 and 1703.

STEP SIX

Tie six full strands of 0601 into a bow.
Stitch the bow onto the bouquet. Embroider a French knot in the same colour for the centre.

MAKING UP

STEP ONE

Trace the outline of the frame onto the
template plastic. Using nail scissors to
achieve a smooth edge, cut around the
outline. The best way to do this is to
keep your hand and the scissors still
while moving the plastic around. Glue
one end of the ribbon to the plastic
frame, then bind the frame with the
length of the ribbon, gluing the end
down on the back to finish.

STEP TWO

Cut the photograph to fit inside the
satin-bound frame. Using the double-
sided tape, stick the photograph into
position. Cover the back of the frame
with double-sided tape and press it
into place over the photograph.

STEP THREE

Stitch the tassel into place. (I stitched
right down the cord and at the back of
the top of the tassel to ensure it was
secure.) Stitch the button into position.
Glue a brooch or charm securely onto
the frame.

STEP FOUR

Have the piece professionally framed.
Ask the framer to use spacers to keep
the button and brooch off the glass.

Tracing Design

Forget-me-not My friend

Embroidery Design

STITCH GUIDE

BULLION STITCH

Bullion stitch is usually the most daunting for new embroiderers, but is worth mastering. Here are a few tips that I think will help.

Always use a straw needle for bullion stitch as it is the same diameter from the tip to the eye. It has no bulge at the eye which ensures even stitches.

Throughout the book, I have indicated the approximate size of the centre bullion to achieve a rose approximately the size of the one in the design. Remember that the first bullion you make for a rose will determine the size of the rose.

Bring the thread through the fabric and make a small back stitch (distance A).

Wrap the thread around the needle as many times as it takes to cover this distance.

Holding the left thumb over the wrapped thread, gently pull the needle through, guiding the wraps off the needle.

Bring the needle back to the starting point and pass it to the back of the work. Bring the needle up at the next stitch to be worked.

Always add extra wraps to allow for a curve or if working around a circle.

FRENCH KNOT

Bring the thread up through the fabric and twist the thread around the needle once or twice (depending on the size required). Place the needle almost at the starting point (not in the same hole) and, holding the thread down with the left thumb, push the needle to the back and gently guide the thread as it passes through the fabric. Bring the needle out again at the position of the next French knot.

LAZY DAISY STITCH

Bring the thread up through the fabric at **A**. Holding the thread down with the left thumb, insert the needle again at **A**. Bring the needle out at **B** and loop the thread around the needle. Anchor it with a tiny stitch. Proceed to the position of the next stitch.

FLY STITCH

Bring the needle up through the fabric at **A**. Take the needle across to **B** and bring it out at **C**. Keep the thread below

the needle and pull the needle through gently. Anchor the loop with a small straight stitch.

CHAIN STITCH

Bring the needle up through the fabric at **A**. Holding the thread down with the left thumb, insert the needle again at **A**. Make a small stitch to **B**, loop the thread around the needle and pull through gently. Reinsert the needle at **B**. Continue making stitches in this way.

STEM STITCH

There are two ways of working stem stitch: with the thread above or with the thread below the needle. I use both.

Bring the needle up at **A** and pass through at **B**, holding the thread above the needle. Bring the needle up at **C** and pass through at **D**. Continue making stitches in this way, bringing the needle halfway back each time.

Work from left to right or bottom to top, making even, slightly slanting stitches along the line to be embroidered. Bring the needle out to the left of the last stitch. Keep the thread below the needle.

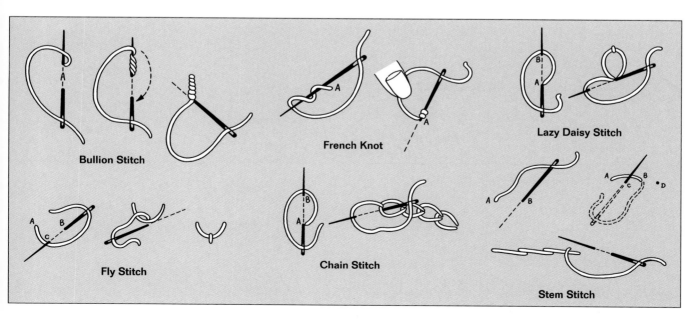

Bullion Stitch

French Knot

Lazy Daisy Stitch

Fly Stitch

Chain Stitch

Stem Stitch

SATIN STITCH

Bring the needle up through the fabric. Work straight stitches, keeping the stitches close together and maintaining a smooth edge.

BACK STITCH

METHOD 1

Bring the needle up at **A** and pass through at **B**, bringing the needle up again at **C**. Come back to the start of the previous stitch. Keep the stitches small and even.

METHOD 2

Bring the thread up through the fabric and make a small back stitch. Bring the needle up again a little in front of the first stitch and make another stitch by taking the needle back to where the last stitch came through.

FEATHER STITCH

Bring the needle up through the fabric on the line to be followed. Take the stitch from the right side back to the centre, with the thread under the needle. Take a stitch on the left side and back to the centre line as before. Continue in this manner.

BUTTONHOLE STITCH

Bring the thread up through the fabric at **A** and pass through at **B**. Bring the needle up again at **C**, close to **A**. Keeping the thread behind the needle, reinsert the needle at **B**, coming up again close to the last stitch. Keep coming back to the same centre point as you work stitches around the circle anticlockwise.

WHIP STITCH

Stitch a row of back stitches. Bring the needle up through the fabric at **A** and pass the needle under the first back stitch, ensuring that the needle does not pass through the fabric. Bring the needle and thread over the back stitch, ready to be passed under the next one. Continue in this manner until all the back stitches are whipped, then pass the thread to the back and finish.

BLANKET STITCH

Work blanket stitch in the same way as buttonhole stitch, but leave a space between the stitches.

RIBBON STITCH

Bring the needle through at **A** and take it to the back, passing it through the ribbon at **B**. Don't pull the ribbon too tightly.

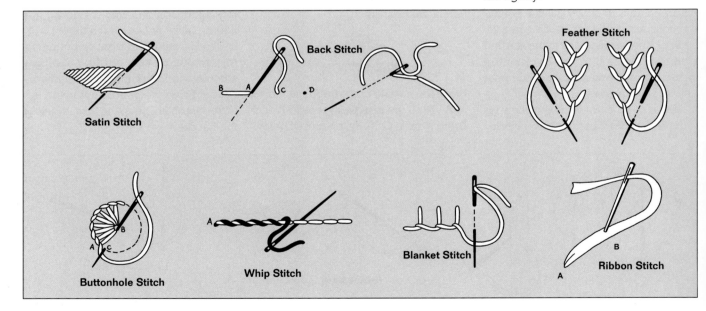

FABRIC

The fabric you choose for your embroidery is entirely optional. In fact, it is always exciting to experiment with new fabrics and textures. I love embroidering on homespun and linen, but silk, moiré, damask, satin and velvet are also beautiful to work with.

If I am going to paint the design to be embroidered, I always choose homespun as it takes the paint so beautifully.

Dark, rich fabrics look stunning embellished with embroidery, but if you need to trace the design, make sure you can see through your fabric when you hold it up to the light. Some dark fabrics, like homespun and silk can be traced onto quite well.

If you are using a fabric which frays readily, bind the edges with tape before you begin. This will save you enormous frustration.

Washable fabric should be washed and pressed dry before embroidering to remove any dressing or sizing from the fabric.

NEEDLES

For all my fine embroidery designs, I use a size 10 straw or crewel needle with one strand of thread. If you wish to use two strands of thread, use a size 8 or 9 needle.

For the ribbon embroidery, I use a size 22 chenille needle for 4 mm (³/₁₆ in) wide ribbon and a size 26 chenille needle for 7 mm (⁵/₁₆ in) wide ribbon.

Straw needles are for working bullion stitch and French knots, but I must confess that I often use the crewel needle for French knots. Straw needles, being the same diameter from the eye to the point, make stitches with no bulge, ensuring more even stitches. I use crewel needles for all the other embroidery stitches.

A most important note: never use damaged, bent or rusty needles.

THREADS

There is an incredible variety of threads available to choose from: cotton, silk, rayon, ribbon and wool. Throughout the book I have used Madeira and DMC threads. In almost all cases both are specified so you can choose which to use.

All the pieces in the book were embroidered with a single strand of thread, unless stated otherwise. To separate one strand, I hold the cotton in my fingertips, pull out one strand and pull it straight up. I pass my fingers down the strand to remove any kinks and thread it into the needle from the bottom end.

When cutting thread for embroidery, always use sharp scissors.

To determine the right length of thread, I measure from my fingertips to my elbow. Longer threads often result in fraying, tangling and frustration.

EMBROIDERY HOOP

I use a hoop only when embroidering satin stitch or wording. For other embroidery, I find a hoop very restrictive and hard to work with. Working without a hoop, I try to keep my stitches a little looser to prevent puckering.

If you are using a hoop, bind the inner ring with cotton tape to avoid marking the fabric. Always remove the hoop when you are not embroidering, to avoid stretching or marking.

EMBROIDERY TIPS

TRACING THE DESIGN

For tracing the designs, use a water-soluble marker pen or a soft lead pencil. I sometimes find the pens a little too thick for fine work, such as wording, and prefer to use a sharp pencil. I make sure the pencil lines will be covered by the embroidery.

If you are lucky enough to have a light box, that is ideal for tracing. Otherwise, tape the design (or a tracing of it) onto a sunny window, then tape the fabric over the tracing. Trace the design onto the fabric in a fine line or a series of dots.

EMBROIDERING

Always wash your hands before beginning to embroider.

It is a good idea to plan the sequence of embroidery before you begin, to avoid moving your hand over finished work as much as possible. I always embroider larger sections first, then fill in with the smaller details. I work from the top to the bottom or from the centre outwards.

Take the time to finish off the thread at the back of the work, instead of passing to another area. This will avoid shadowing which is very disappointing when the finished work is framed or made up. However, when I am working on very closely embroidered areas, I do pass the thread across as it will not be visible.

You may enjoy adding small beads to enhance your embroidery. They can be sprinkled among the flowers or form the centre of a flower. Small buttons may also be used. There are some wonderful tiny buttons available – some even shaped like flowers. Take care to keep the buttons in proportion to the design so as not to distort the dimensions.

If you wish to add embellishments and also to 'age' your embroidery, dye the piece first following the instructions on page 80.

WASHING FABRIC

The finished embroidery should be rinsed gently in lukewarm water. I add a few drops of white vinegar to restore lustre to the threads.

Press the piece dry by placing it face down on a towel with a piece of linen over the top. I keep a linen teatowel especially for the purpose. Press gently until the embroidery is dry. It is very important to press dry in this way; leaving your embroidery to dry naturally may result in the colours bleeding.

Always wash the fabric before dyeing to age it. Otherwise any marks will become permanent. If there is a mark, washing it in a wool wash and rinsing thoroughly will be quite successful.

AGING AND DYEING FABRIC

If you wish to age your embroidery, dye it in coffee, either before or after embroidering. I like the effect of dyeing after embroidering – it does not change the colour of the threads, but mutes them a little.

To dye fabric: make up a mixture of five cups of boiling water with five dessertspoons of coffee, mixed well. Soak the embroidery in this mixture for fifteen to twenty minutes, then rinse it in clean lukewarm water. Soak it for another few minutes in clean lukewarm water with a few drops of white vinegar added.

FRAMING

The designs in this book can be used in many ways: framing, cushions, patchwork, wallhangings – just to name a few. I have chosen to frame most of mine because it makes exhibiting them so much easier.

It is very important to choose the framer carefully. Make sure the framer will stretch and pin the piece and use acid-free backing board. If you have embellished your work with buttons and beads, ask the framer to use spacers when the piece is framed. If you have combined your embroidery with mementoes, a box frame is a good idea.

Whether or not you use glass in the frame is a matter of personal choice. The texture of the work is enhanced if there is no glass; on the other hand, glass will protect the embroidery from dust or damage.

SIGNING AND DATING

Always sign and date your finished piece – your full name or initials. I prefer to embroider my name or initials, KAE, and the date but on some pieces, such as the painted ones, I have used a waterproof pen.

On some pieces it is difficult to know where to place the name so it does not detract from the design. When this occurs, I sign and date the pieces somewhere out of sight (such as under the frame). Though it is not immediately visible, the signature is still there for posterity.

ACKNOWLEDGMENTS

Over the past few months, while preparing for this book, I have been blessed with great support from my wonderful family and friends.

To Peter, Cameron, Nita, Shannon and Rob, the trust and faith you have all shown in my abilities has been truly appreciated. I would never have had this opportunity if it were not for your patience, support and help. Thank you Pete for your total commitment to my work. I hope one day I can repay you for your dedication; words never seem to be enough.

For many years, Diane Partridge has been an important part of our lives and is always there when she is needed. Her loyalty, understanding and high standards are invaluable to both our family and to Kae's Treasures and Heirlooms.

So often I turn to my friend Julie Healy for her opinion and advice. Sometimes the matter seems so trivial, but it is always important. Julie's honesty, patience, encouragement and friendship keep me going when I have times of self-doubt.

My special thanks go to my framer, Raelene Van Zyl from Conserve Framing. Her skill, advice and friendship is very much appreciated.

After I finished embroidering some of the pieces, they were beautifully made up by Lois Johnson – a very talented woman who gives so much of herself to any project she undertakes.

Thank you to Daryl Craze from Penguin Threads for supplying the Madeira threads. I appreciate his support and kindness.

Lastly, my heartfelt thanks and gratitude to Judy Poulos for inviting me to write this book. It has been a great privilege and a wonderful experience.